**THE ROYAL COURT
THEATRE PRESENTS**

LINDA

by Penelope Skinner

Linda was first p
Jerwood Theatre
on Thursday 26th

LINDA
by Penelope Skinner

CAST (in alphabetical order)

Bridget **Imogen Byron**
Alice **Karla Crome**
Luke **Jaz Deol**
Linda **Noma Dumezweni**
Amy **Amy Beth Hayes**
Neil **Dominic Mafham**
Stevie **Merriel Plummer**
Dave **Ian Redford**

Director **Michael Longhurst**
Set Designer **Es Devlin**
Costume Designer **Alex Lowde**
Video Designer **Luke Halls**
Lighting Designer **Lee Curran**
Composer & Sound Designer **Richard Hammarton**
Movement Director **Imogen Knight**
Voice & Dialect Coach **Penny Dyer**
Casting Director **Amy Ball**
Associate Director **Katy Rudd**
Production Manager **Matt Noddings**
Fight Director **Bret Yount**
Stage Manager **Michael Dennis**
Deputy Stage Manager **Sarah Hellicar**
Assistant Stage Manager **Osnat Koblenz**
Stage Management Placement **Samantha Leese**
Set built by **Scott Fleary**

The Royal Court & Stage Management wish to thank the following for their help with this
production: Nigel Lilley, Machiko Weston, Bronia Housman, Jed Skrzypczak and Angie Vasileiou

LINDA
by Penelope Skinner

Penelope Skinner (Writer)

For the Royal Court: **The Village Bike.**

Other theatre includes: **Fred's Diner (Magic, San Francisco); The Village Bike (MCC, New York); The Promise (Donmar/Trafalgar Studios); Fred's Diner (Chichester Festival); The Sound of Heavy Rain (Paines Plough); Greenland (National); Eigengrau (Bush); Fucked (Assembly, Edinburgh/Old Red Lion).**

Television includes: **Fresh Meat.**

Film includes: **Mary Stuart, How I Live Now.**

Radio includes: **Planet B, The Man in Black, Scratch, Murder in the Toilet.**

Awards include: **George Devine Award, Evening Standard Theatre Awards Charles Wintour Most Promising Playwright (The Village Bike).**

Imogen Byron (Bridget)

Theatre includes: **Pride & Prejudice, The Wind In The Willows (Regent's Park Open Air); That Face (Landor); Inherit the Wind (Old Vic); Feather Boy (National); Evita, Les Misérables (West End).**

Television includes: **Grantchester, Holby City, The Omid Djalili Show, That Mitchell & Webb Look, Cranford, Waking The Dead, Forgiven, Home Again, Green Wing, Messiah, Stupid Comedy Sketch Show, Hardware, Murphy's Law.**

Film includes: **Last Chance Harvey, Pickles, Tunnel of Love.**

Karla Crome (Alice)

Theatre includes: **Powder Monkey (Royal Exchange, Manchester).**

Televison includes: **You, Me & the Apocalypse, Under the Dome, Prisoners' Wives, Lightfields, Misfits, Murder, Monroe, Hit & Miss, Doctors, Casualty.**

Lee Curran (Lighting Designer)

For the Royal Court: **Constellations (& West End/Broadway).**

Other Theatre includes: **Splendour (Donmar); The Oresteia (Home, Manchester); Love's Sacrifice, Arden of Faversham (RSC); Hamlet, Much Ado About Nothing, Blindsided (Royal Exchange, Manchester); Mametz (National Theatre Wales); Protest Song (National); A Number (Nuffield/Young Vic); Regeneration, Dancing at Lughnasa (Northampton); Blam! (Neander); The Jungle Book (West Yorkshire Playhouse); Turfed, 66 minutes in Damascus (LIFT); The Sacred Flame (ETT/Rose, Kingston); The Fat Girl Gets A Haircut & Other Stories, Puffball (Roundhouse) The Rise & Shine of Comrade Fiasco, Unbroken (Gate); Clytemnestra (Sherman Cymru); The Empty Quarter (Hampstead).**

Dance includes: **Sun, Political Mother, The Art of Not Looking Back, In Your Rooms, Uprising (Hofesh Schecter); Untouchable (Royal Ballet); Frames, Curious Conscience (Rambert); The Measures Taken, All That is Solid Melts into Air, The Grit in the Oyster (Alexander Whitley); Bastard Amber, Interloper (Liz Roche); There We Have Been (James Cousins); Wide Awakening (Joss Arnott); The Letter (Jonzi D); E2 7SD, Soledad, Voices & Set Boundaries, Rafael (Bonachela).**

Opera includes: **Orpheé et Eurydice (ROH); Nabucco (Opera National de lorraine); Ottone, Life On The Moon (English Touring Opera).**

Jaz Deol (Luke)

For the Royal Court: **The Djinns of Eidgar.**

Other theatre include: **Mush & Me (Bush/Edinburgh Fringe Festival/Camden Peoples); Speed (Kali); Harlesden High Street (Tara Arts/Jackdaw); Snookered (Tamasha); Snow Queen (International tour); Ruffled (503); King Lear (Young Vic).**

Television includes: **Together, Code of a Killer.**

Film includes: **Viceroy's House, The Show, Honeycomb Lodge, Cleanskin, Haraam Chai (& writer).**

Radio includes: **Recent Events at Collington House, Karma, An Everyday Story of Afghan Folk, Salman Taooor, Trojan Horse.**

Awards include: **Twice awarded Triforce Promotions Three Minute Monologue Slam Award for Best Actor.**

Es Devlin (Set Designer)

For the Royal Court: **The Nether (& West End); Dumb Show, O Go My Man, Credible Witness, Yard Gal.**

Other theatre includes: **Hamlet (Barbican); Light Shining in Buckinghamshire (National); Machinal (Roundabout, New York); Chimerica (Almeida/West End); American Psycho, Five Gold Rings (Almeida); A Midsummer Night's Dream (Theatre for a New Audience, New York); Robin des Bois (Palais de Congres); The Master & Margarita (Complicité/tour); Batman (International tour); Pieces of Vincent, Macbeth (Arcola); Hecuba, Spanish Golden Age Season, Antony & Cleopatra, Henry IV Parts 1&2, The Prisoner's Dilemma (RSC); Betrayal, Hinterland (National); A Day in the Death of Joe Egg (West End/Broadway); Hamlet (Young Vic); Snake in the Grass (Old Vic); On Ego, Rita, Sue & Bob Too, A State Affair, Arabian Night (Soho); The Death of Cool (Hampstead); Airsick, One life & Counting, Love You Too, Howie the Rookie, Love & Understanding (Bush); Perapalas (Gate); All the Ordinary Angels (Royal Exchange, Manchester); Meat (Theatre Royal, Plymouth); Piano (Theatre Project Tokyo); Edward II (Octagon, Bolton).**

Dance includes: **Connectome, New Work by Alastair Marriot (Royal Ballet); Rodin Project, After Light II, After Light I, Small Boats, God's Plenty, Four Scenes (Rambert); Blaze (Peacock); Essence (ROH); I Remember Red (Cullberg Ballet, Stockholm); A Streetcar Named Desire (Northern Ballet).**

Opera Includes: **Otello (Metroplitan, New York); The Rise and Fall of the City of Mahagonny, Don Giovanni, Les Troyens, Lucrezia Borgia, Salome (ROH); Beatrice et Benedict (Theater an der Wien); Imago, Knight Crew (Glyndebourne); Parsifal, The Cunning Little Vixen (Royal Danish Opera); Die Tote Stadt (Finnish National Opera); Faust (Dresden SemperOper); I Puritani (De Nederlandse Opera).**

Concert Design includes: **Innocence + Experience for U2, Yeezus, Glow in the Dark, Touch the Sky for Kanye West, Watch the Throne for Kanye West & Jay Z, Monsterball (US theatre version) for Lady Gaga, Resistance for Muse, Electric, Pandemonium & Fundamental for Pet Shop Boys, Ellipse for Imogen Heap, Head First for Goldfrapp, Bangerz for Miley Cyrus.**

Awards include: **Olivier Award for Best Set Design (The Nether); Critics' Circle Award for Best Designer (Chimerica);** Total Production International Award for Set Designer of the Year; Red Magazine Creative Woman of the Year; Olivier Award for Best Costume Design (The Dog in the Manger); Manchester Evening News Theatre Award for Best Design (Beautiful Thing); The Linbury Prize for Stage Design.

Es Devlin was the designer for the London 2012 Olympic Closing Ceremony. She was awarded the OBE in 2015.

Noma Dumezweni (Linda)

For the Royal Court: **Feast (Young Vic), Belong.**

Other theatre includes: **A Human Being Died that Night (Brooklyn Academy of Music/ Hampstead/Fugard & Market Theatres, South Africa); Carmen Disruption (Almeida); 'Tis Pity She's A Whore (Globe); A Walk on Part–The Fall of New Labour (Soho); The Winter's Tale, Julius Caesar, The Grainstore, Morte D'Arthur, Romeo & Juliet, Little Eagles, Macbeth (RSC); Six Characters in Search of an Author (Chichester Festival/West End); The Master & Margarita, Nathan the Wise, The Coffee House (Chichester Festival); The Hour We Knew Nothing of Each Other, President of an Empty Room (National); Breakfast with Mugabe (RSC/Soho/ West End); A Raisin in the Sun (Lyric Hammersmith/West End/Tour); Skellig (Young Vic); Henry V, Anthony & Cleopatra, Much Ado About Nothing (West End); The Bogus Woman (Red Room/Bush).**

Television includes: **Casualty, Capital, The Marriage of Reason & Squalor, Midsomer Murders, Frankie, Doctor Who, Summerhill, The Colour of Magic, The Last Enemy, Together, Fallout, Little Miss Jocelyn, EastEnders, New Tricks, Holby City, Fallen Angel, After Thomas, Silent Witness.**

Film includes: **The Incident, Dirty Pretty Things, Macbeth.**

Awards include: **Olivier Award for Best Supporting Performer (A Raisin in the Sun); Fringe First, Manchester Evening News Award (The Bogus Woman).**

Penny Dyer
(Voice & Dialect Coach)

For the Royal Court: **The Wolf From The Door, The Mistress Contract, Circle Mirror Transformation, The Low Road, Choir Boy, In Basildon, Posh (& West End), Clybourne Park (& West End), Remembrance Day, The Faith Machine, The Girlfriend Experience, Chicken Soup with Barley, Aunt Dan &**

Lemon, The Fever, Tusk Tusk, Wig Out!, The Pride, Now or Later, The Vertical Hour, Redundant, Plasticine, Spinning into Butter, Fireface, Other People, Mojo.

Other theatre includes: **Husbands & Sons, This House, Blood & Gifts** (National); **Teddy Ferrara** (Donmar); **The Ruling Class** (Trafalgar Studios); **Gypsy** (CFT/SAVOY); **Assassins** (Menier Chocolate Factory); **Sweet Bird of Youth, Speed-the-Plow** (Old Vic); **The Michael Grandage Company Season, The Commitments, The Book of Mormon, Abigail's Party, Absent Friends, Legally Blond** (West End); **Desire Under the Elms, Saved, Spring Awakening** (Lyric, Hammersmith); **Good People, 55 Days** (Hampstead), **Julius Caesar** (RSC); **A Delicate Balance, Becky Shaw** (Almeida); **Roots, The Promise, Salt, Root & Roe, Anna Christie, Spelling Bee, Passion, A Streetcar Named Desire, Small Changes, Parade, Piaf, Frost/Nixon, After Miss Julie, The Blue Room** (Donmar); **How To Succeed In Business** (Broadway).

Film includes: **Florence Foster Jenkins, The Danish Girl, The Jungle Book, Dad's Army, Testament of Youth, Pride, Philomena, Sunshine on Leith, Kill My Darlings, My Week with Marilyn, Tamara Drewe, Nowhere Boy, The Damned United, The Queen, Frost/Nixon, Infamous, Dirty Pretty Things, Ladies in Lavender, Elizabeth.**

Television includes: **Marvellous, The Last Kingdom, The Missing, Code of a Killer, Cilla, Tubby & Enid, Tommy Cooper, The Girl, Mrs Biggs, The Job Lot, The Slap, Downton Abbey, Gracie, Small Island, Margaret, Most Sincerely, Fantabuloso, The Deal.**

Luke Halls (Video Designer)

For the Royal Court: **The Nether (& West End), 2071.**

Other theatre includes: **Man & Superman** (National); **Hamlet** (Barbican); **Miss Saigon, I Can't Sing!** (West End); **Mary Poppins** (UK tour); **The Master & Margarita** (Complicité/tour).

Dance includes: **Connectome** (Royal Ballet); **Zeitgeist** (Coliseum).

Opera includes: **Otello** (Metropolitan Opera, New York); **Król Roger, Don Giovanni** (ROH); **Der Freischütz, The Cunning Little Vixen** (Danish Royal Opera).

Live music tours include: **Pet Shop Boys** (Turn It On, Pandemonium, Axis World Tour); **U2** (360, Vertigo); **Muse** (Resistance); **Rolling Stones** (A Bigger Bang); **George Michael** (25); **Robbie Williams** (Take The Crown); **Take That** (Beautiful World); **Genesis** (Turn It On Again).

Awards include: **Knight of Illumination Award** (Don Giovanni); **BAFTA Award for Entertainment Craft Team** (The Cube).

Luke has created video designs for live music performances by Rhianna, Pet Shop Boys, Elton John, U2 & Nitin Sawhney. He was the video designer for the closing ceremonies of the London 2012 Paralympic & Olympic Games.

Richard Hammarton
(Composer & Sound Designer)

Theatre includes: **The Crucible, Brilliant Adventures, Edward II, Dr Faustus** (Royal Exchange, Manchester); **Deposit, Faultlines** (Hampstead); **Comrade Fiasco** (Gate); **Grimm Tales 2** (Bargehouse, Oxo Tower Wharf); **Beached** (Marlowe/Soho); **Ghost From a Perfect Place, The Pitchfork Disney** (Arcola); **The Crucible** (Old Vic); **Dealer's Choice** (Royal & Derngate); **Kingston 14** (Theatre Royal, Stratford East); **A Number** (Nuffield/Young Vic); **Early Days (Of a Better Nation)** (BAC); **Sizwe Bansi Is Dead** (Young Vic/tour); **An Inspector Calls** (Theatre By the Lake); **Bandages** (TEG Productions); **The Last Summer** (Gate, Dublin); **Mudlarks** (HighTide Festival/503/Bush); **The Taming of the Shrew** (Globe); **Judgement Day** (Print Room); **Same Same, Little Baby Jesus, Fixer** (Oval House); **Persuasion, The Constant Wife, Les Liasons Dangereuses, Arsenic & Old Lace, The Real Thing, People At Sea** (Salisbury Playhouse); **Platform** (Old Vic Tunnels); **Ghosts, Speaking in Tongues** (West End); **Pride & Prejudice** (Theatre Royal, Bath/tour); **The Mountain Top** (503/West End); **The Rise & Fall of Little Voice** (Harrogate); **A Raisin in the Sun** (Lyric, Hammersmith/tour); **The Shooky, Dealer's Choice** (Young Vic); **Breakfast With Mugabe** (Theatre Royal, Bath); **Someone Who'll Watch Over Me** (Theatre Royal, Northampton); **Inches Apart, Natural Selection, Salt Meets Wound, Ship of Fools** (503).

Television includes: **Ripper Street, Agatha Christie's Marple, No Win No Fee, Sex 'N' Death, Wipeout, The Ship, Konigsspitz, K2, The Fisherman's Wife.**

Awards include: **Manchester Evening News Award for Best Design** (Dr Faustus).

Amy Beth Hayes (Amy)

Theatre includes: **Les Liaisons Dangereuses** (RSC); **Jerusalem** (West End); **True Love**

Lies (Royal Exchange, Manchester); On The Waterfront (Hackney Empire).

Television includes: **Mr Selfridge, Lilyhammer, The Syndicate, Shameless, Sirens, Case Sensitive, Secret Diary of a Call Girl, Misfits, Syntax Era, FM, Whatever It Takes, The Children, Harry & Paul, Doctor Who, No Heroics.**

Film includes: **Eva, Watermarks, Me Me Me, Captcha.**

Radio includes: **Journey To Starlight Mountain, Maurice.**

Imogen Knight (Movement Director)

For the Royal Court: **God Bless the Child, Pests (& Clean Break/Royal Exchange, Manchester/UK tour), Love, Love, Love, The Low Road, A Time to Reap.**

Other Theatre Includes: **I Want My Hat Back, Edward II, Dido, Queen of Carthage (National); Measure for Measure, Dirty Butterfly (Young Vic); Our Ladies of Perpetual Succour, In Time O'Strife, An Appointment with the Wicker Man, The Missing (National Theatre of Scotland); The Skriker (Manchester International Festival /Royal Exchange, Manchaester); Carmen Disruption, Little Revolution, Turn Of The Screw, King Lear, Filumena, Measure For Measure, When The Rain Stops Falling, Marianne Dreams (Almeida); The Broken Heart, 'Tis Pity She's A Whore (Globe); Hamlet, Blindsided, Cannibals (Royal Exchange, Manchester); The Crucible (Old Vic); Arden Of Faversham (RSC); Of Mice & Men, As You Like It (West Yorkshire Playhouse); Red Velvet (Tricycle/St Anne's Warehouse, New York); The History Boys, Macbeth (Sheffield Crucible); but i cd only whisper, When Five Years Pass (Arcola); One Day When We Were Young, The Sound Of Heavy Rain (Paines Plough); The Tempest (Watermill); Persuasion (Salisbury Playhouse); Corrie (Lowry/UK tour); Snow Queen (Chichester Festival); The Boiler Room (Clean Break); A Doll's House (Exeter Northcott); Wuthering Heights (Birmingham Rep); Success (National with Islington Youth).**

Dance Includes: **Under the Carpet (De Stilte, Holland); OMG! (Sadler's Wells/Company of Angels/The Place); Penelope (Dramaturgs Network/Company of Angels).**

Opera Includes: **Powder Her Face (English National Opera); How To Make An Opera, The Little Sweep (Malmo).**

Television includes: **The Hollow Crown, Call the Midwife, My Name Is Ruthie Segal, Hear Me Roar.**

Imogen was previously an Associate Artist with Frantic Assembly, she is also a guest lecturer in Movement at Central School of Speech and Drama.

Michael Longhurst (Director)

For the Royal Court: **Constellations (& West End/Broadway/UK tour), The Art of Dying, Remembrance Day.**

Other theatre includes: **A Number (National/Nuffield); Carmen Disruption (Almeida), 'Tis Pity She's a Whore (Sam Wanamaker), Bad Jews (Ustinov/St James/West End/UK tour); Dealer's Choice (Royal & Derngate); The Blackest Black (Hampstead); The World of Extreme Happiness (National); Cannibals (Royal Exchange, Manchester); The History Boys (Crucible, Sheffield); If There Is I Haven't Found It Yet (Roundabout, New York); 66 Books (Bush); Midnight Your Time (HighTide/Assembly Rooms Edinburgh); On the Record (Arcola); It's About Time (Latitude) On the Beach (Bush); Dirty Butterfly (Young Vic); Stovepipe (HighTide/Bush/National); Gaudeamus (Arcola); Cargo (Oval House); Guardian (Pleasance, Edinburgh/503); Doctor Faustus (Lakeside Arts Centre, Nottingham).**

Awards include: **Evening Standard Award for Best Play (Constellations); Jerwood Directors Award at the Young Vic (Dirty Butterfly); Fringe First Award (Guardians).**

Alex Lowde (Costume Designer)

Theatre includes: **Miss Julie (Aarhus); Game (Almeida); 'Tis Pity She's a Whore (Globe); Krapp's Last Tape (Sheffield); Edward II (National); Enjoy (West Yorkshire Playhouse); The Body of an American (Gate); Lines, Stink Foot (The Yard); The Glass Menagerie, A Doll's House, Anna Karenina, Beauty & the Beast, She Town, The Elephant Man, Equus (Dundee Rep); A Christmas Carol, Takin' Over the Asylum, The Marriage of Figaro (Lyceum, Edinburgh); Innocence (Scottish Dance); Carousel (Royal Conservatoire of Scotland); Blake Diptych (Laban); Victoria Station/One for the Road (Print Room/Young Vic); A Clockwork Orange (Theatre Royal, Stratford East); While You Lie (Traverse).**

Opera includes: **Rigoletto (Opera Theatre Company Wexford/Irish tour); The Adventures of Mr Broucek (Opera North/Scottish Opera); Tobias & the Angel (Young**

Vic); The Lion's Face, The Nose (The Opera Group/ROH2); Paradise Moscow (Royal Academy of Music); The Gentle Giant (ROH2); Le Nozze di Figaro (Sadler's Wells).

Awards include: **Critics Award for Theatre Design in Scotland (Beauty & the Beast); Critics Award for Theatre Design in Scotland (The Elephant Man).**

Dominic Mafham (Neil)

Theatre includes: **The Merchant of Venice (Globe); 66 Books – A Response To Daniel (Bush); Journey's End (West End/tour); Four Nights in Knaresborough (West Yorkshire Playhouse); Three Sisters (Nuffield/National); Nabokov's Gloves (Hampstead); Edward II, Richard II, A Jovial Crew, Anthony & Cleopatra (RSC).**

Television includes: **Father Brown, Humans, New Tricks, The Musketeers, Nixon's The One, Lewis, DCI Banks, Land Girls, Midsomer Murders, The Clinic, Kingdom, The Queen's Sister, Red Cap, Rose & Maloney, Spooks, Henry VIII, Dalziel & Pascoe, Foyles War, State of Mind, Gentleman's Relish, Always & Everyone, Our Mutual Friend, The Fragile Heart.**

Film includes: **Sniper 6: Kill Shot, Sniper 5: Remote Control, Dragonheart: Druid's Curse, Heart of Lightness, Dungeons & Dragons 3, The Waiting Room, Hard Labour, Shooting Fish, The English Patient.**

Merriel Plummer (Stevie)

Theatre includes: **Robin Hood, Sticks & Stones, Escape, Binge, The HOPE Play (Saltmine).**

Awards include: **TriForce Promotions One Minute Monologue Slam Award for Best Actor.**

Ian Redford (Dave)

For the Royal Court: **Bruises, Built on Sand, William, The Plague Year, Irish Eyes & English Tears.**

Other theatre includes: **Mad World My Master, The Roaring Girl, Arden of Faversham, The Witch of Edmonton, Candide (RSC); All My Sons (Leicester Curve); A View From The Bridge, The Gatekeeper, Dr Faustus, Antigone (Royal Exchange, Manchester); A Dish of Tea with Dr Johnson (& co-writer), Rita, Sue & Bob Too!, A State Affair, The Permanent Way, Some Explicit Polaroid, Our Country's Good, Shopping & Fucking, A Laughing Matter (Out of Joint); Robin Hood (Cambridge Arts); Brimstone & Treacle (Arcola); Six Degrees**

Of Separation (Old Vic); Helen, Romeo & Juliet (Globe); She Stoops To Conquer, Free, Love The Sinner, Mother Clap's Molly House (National); Tiger Tail (Drum); Chapter Two, Madame Butterfly (West End); Agammemnon's Children (Gate); Whose Life Is It Anyway?, The Merchant of Venice (Birmingham Rep).

Televison includes: **New Tricks, Henry VIII, The Devil's Whore, Heartbeat, Doctors, The Chase, Party Animals, Animals, Coronation Street, Derailed, Missing, William & Mary, Regicide, The Prince & The Pauper, Trial By Fire, Second Sight, One Foot In The Grave, Animal Ark, Stone Scissors Paper, Wycliffe, Family Style, I.D., House of Elliot, Foyle's War, Statement of Affairs, The Bill, Moon & Son, The Men's Room, Medics, Van Der Valk, Antonia & Jane, Minder, Thin Air, EastEnders, Bust, Dramarama.**

Film includes: **HHHH, Mary & Martha, The Legend of Boogeyman 4, She Stoops To Conquer, Remains of the Day, Just Like a Woman, Three Men & A Little Lady, Getting It Right, The Great Escape.**

Katy Rudd (Associate Director)

For the Royal Court, as Associate Director: **The Twits.**

As Director, theatre includes: **A Curious Night at the Theatre (West End); I'm Really Glad We Had that Chat (Arcola); Henna Night (Edinburgh International Festival); The Butterfly (Salisbury); Narcissus (Edge, Leeds); The 24 Hour Plays: New Voices (Old Vic); Hippolytus (Stage@Leeds); Shafted (NCM Museum).**

As Associate Director, theatre includes: **Husbands & Sons (National/Royal Exchange, Manchester); The Curious Incident of the Dog in the Night-Time (National/West End/Broadway/tour).**

As Assistant Director, theatre includes: **Mathematics of the Heart (503); 24 Hour Plays Gala Performance, The Playboy of the Western World (Old Vic); Bed & Sofa (Finborough); The Constant Wife, The Family Cookbook (Salisbury); Into the Woods (Regent's Park Open Air).**

THE ROYAL COURT THEATRE

The Royal Court Theatre is the writers' theatre. It is the leading force in world theatre for energetically cultivating writers – undiscovered, new, and established.

Through the writers the Royal Court is at the forefront of creating restless, alert, provocative theatre about now, inspiring audiences and influencing future writers. Through the writers the Royal Court strives to constantly reinvent the theatre ecology, creating theatre for everyone.

We invite and enable conversation and debate, allowing writers and their ideas to reach and resonate beyond the stage, and the public to share in the thinking.

Over 120,000 people visit the Royal Court in Sloane Square, London, each year and many thousands more see our work elsewhere through transfers to the West End and New York, national and international tours, residencies across London and site-specific work.

The Royal Court's extensive development activity encompasses a diverse range of writers and artists and includes an ongoing programme of writers' attachments, readings, workshops and playwriting groups. Twenty years of pioneering work around the world means the Royal Court has relationships with writers on every continent.

The Royal Court opens its doors to radical thinking and provocative discussion, and to the unheard voices and free thinkers that, through their writing, change our way of seeing.

Within the past sixty years, John Osborne, Arnold Wesker and Howard Brenton have all started their careers at the Court. Many others, including Caryl Churchill, Mark Ravenhill and Sarah Kane have followed. More recently, the theatre has found and fostered new writers such as Polly Stenham, Mike Bartlett, Bola Agbaje, Nick Payne and Rachel De-lahay and produced many iconic plays from Laura Wade's **Posh** to Bruce Norris' **Clybourne Park** and Jez Butterworth's **Jerusalem**. Royal Court plays from every decade are now performed on stage and taught in classrooms across the globe.

It is because of this commitment to the writer that we believe there is no more important theatre in the world than the Royal Court.

Supported using public funding by
ARTS COUNCIL ENGLAND

ROYAL COURT SUPPORTERS

The Royal Court is a registered charity and not-for-profit company. We need to raise £1.7 million every year in addition to our core grant from the Arts Council and our ticket income to achieve what we do.

We have significant and longstanding relationships with many generous organisations and individuals who provide vital support. Royal Court supporters enable us to remain the writers' theatre, find stories from everywhere and create theatre for everyone.

We can't do it without you.

Innovation partner

Supported using public funding by
**ARTS COUNCIL
ENGLAND**

The Royal Court works with a huge variety of companies ranging from small local businesses to large global firms. The Court has been at the cutting edge of new drama for more than 50 years and, situated in the heart of Chelsea, makes the perfect evening for a night of unique client entertaining.

By becoming a Business Member, your company will be given an allocation of London's hottest tickets with the chance of booking in for sold out shows, the opportunity to entertain your clients in our stunning Balcony Bar and exclusive access to the creative members of staff and cast members.

BECOME A BUSINESS MEMBER

To discuss Business Membership at the Royal Court, please contact:
Nadia Vistisen, Development Officer
nadiavistisen@royalcourttheatre.com
020 7565 5030

The English Stage Company at the Royal Court Theatre is a registered charity (No. 231242).

Linda

Penelope Skinner's plays include *Fred's Diner* (Chichester
Festival 'Pop Up' Theatre, 2012), *The Promise* by Aleksei
Arbuzov (adaptation for the Donmar Warehouse / Trafalgar
Studios, 2012), *The Village Bike* (Royal Court Upstairs,
2011), *The Sound of Heavy Rain* (Paines Plough / Crucible
Theatre, Sheffield, 2011), *Greenland* (co-writer, National,
2011), *Eigengrau* (Bush Theatre, 2010), and *Fucked*
(Old Red Lion, 2008; Assembly Rooms, Edinburgh, 2009).
For *The Village Bike* she was the recipient of the 2011
George Devine Award and the 2011 Evening Standard
Charles Wintour Award for Most Promising Playwright.

also by Penelope Skinner from Faber

EIGENGRAU
THE VILLAGE BIKE
THE SOUND OF HEAVY RAIN

PENELOPE SKINNER

Linda

FABER & FABER

First published in 2015
by Faber and Faber Limited
74–77 Great Russell Street, London WC1B 3DA

Typeset by Country Setting, Kingsdown, Kent CT14 8ES
Printed in England by CPI Group (UK) Ltd, Croydon CR0 4YY

A CIP record for this book is available from the British Library

ISBN 978-0-571-33001-0

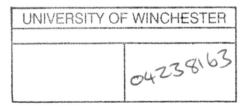
2 4 6 8 10 9 7 5 3 1

For my mother

Acknowledgements

Michael Longhurst. Noma Dumezweni, Karla Crome,
Imogen Byron, Amy Beth Hayes, Ian Redford, Jaz Deol,
Dominic Mafham and Merriel Plummer, aka The Cast.
Giles Smart at United Agents and Scott Chaloff at WME.
Polly Findlay. Kim Cattrall. Vicky Featherstone and Chris
Campbell at the Royal Court. Lynne Meadow and
Elizabeth Rothman at the Manhattan Theatre Club. Katy
Rudd. Sarah Hellicar. Rebecca Huntley for the research.
Aaron Paterson for the title brainstorms. To everyone
who did a reading of this play, especially Kate Duchêne,
Debra Gillett, Tricia Kelly, Helen Schlesinger, Sophie
Stanton, Imogen Stubbs, Meera Syal and Max Baker.
Thank you to my family, and to my fellow 'female writers',
E.V. Crowe, Abby Ajayi and Laura Lomas, for endless
creative support and encouragement.

Linda was first performed at the Royal Court Jerwood
Theatre Downstairs, London, on 26 November 2015.
The cast, in alphabetical order, was as follows:

Bridget Imogen Byron
Alice Karla Crome
Luke Jaz Deol
Linda Noma Dumezweni
Amy Amy Beth Hayes
Neil Dominic Mafham
Stevie Merriel Plummer
Dave Ian Redford

Director Michael Longhurst
Set Designer Es Devlin
Costume Designer Alex Lowde
Video Designer Luke Halls
Lighting Designer Lee Curran
Composer and Sound Designer Richard Hammarton
Movement Director Imogen Knight
Voice and Dialect Coach Penny Dyer

Characters

Linda
female, fifty-five

Alice
female, twenty-five

Bridget
female, fifteen

Neil
male, fifty-four

Amy
female, twenty-five

Stevie
female, twenty-eight

Luke
male, thirty

Dave
male, sixty

LINDA

Act One

ONE

The boardroom of the Swan Beauty Corporation.
Linda is giving a presentation.

She has some pertinent slides.
It takes her a moment to get them working. Then:

Linda So I started off thinking about the research
feedback which always comes in when we do age-related
stuff from women in the over-fifties category about how
    when women get to fifty or somewhere around that
age bracket
    they start to feel invisible. Over and over again in
groups we hear the same thing. 'I feel like life is
happening all around me. I used to be the protagonist of
my life and now suddenly I'm starting to feel irrelevant.'
This can also be connected to women's sexuality, so
    'Men walk past me in the street and don't look twice
any more' or 'I go past a building site and nobody
whistles'. Even in the workplace. Women start to
experience people talking over them. As though what
they are saying is actually less important, because they
have reached a certain age. They also find themselves
under-represented in media – books, films, on television.
And in advertising. The simple truth is that as a woman
in the fifty-plus age group you rarely get marketed to.
Products you might want to buy – and an anti-ageing
cream is a good standard example – are marketed to you
using models in their thirties – reminding you not of who
you could be
    but of who you were twenty years ago. On the few
occasions you do see a woman of your actual age group
in an advert

15

she's either Helen Mirren (the only older woman still allowed to exist) or – she's selling you meals on wheels. She's telling you not to worry because someone's made a pad to keep your pants dry if you find you start to pee involuntarily. She doesn't represent your real life. Your actual concerns. You know I don't mind telling you all that I'm fifty-five years old and I'm not thinking about how big my coffin needs to be. Not just yet!

So to coincide with the launch of this new and exciting product

I would like us

as a company

to start doing the same work for these women as we do for girls. Seven million young women worldwide have benefited from our workshops. Our online toolkits have been accessed by over a million parents. And as award-winning leaders in this field it is my belief that we now owe it to these older women to recognise their plight. Let's make these invisible women feel seen again. Lets say to them: ladies? We know you're out there! We see you! You exist!

She clicks to the final slide – a large logo for 'VISIBILITY'.

TWO

Spotlight on Stevie, standing at a mic. Music plays.

But when it's time to come in, she misses her cue.
    The music carries on for a bit.

Stevie Shit! I missed it. Sorry! Can we go again? From the top?

THREE

Home. Evening.

Neil sits at the table, a laptop open in front of him, an iPhone on the table, tapping on his iPad.
    Bridget, in her school uniform, is setting the table.

Bridget Mr Christian said I should stick with it but Mrs Pargiter says I should try and find something more original. She says girls always end up doing the same three or four speeches because in Shakespeare time girls weren't allowed to act or speak or something? But I looked at everything we've got in the school library and it's not just Shakespeare time. It's everything after that too. Girls hardly ever say anything! You'd have to like cobble a speech together from different little lines and it's not the same because they never talk about anything important. And I said this to Mr Christian. I said it's not just Shakespeare and he said he had a theory about that. And his theory is that when you watch a story about 'men' you know the stakes are really high? Because men might like

actually kill each other? Whereas when you watch a story about a 'woman' it's more like

what's at stake is more like

'When is she going to get married?' Like, superficial? Then Mrs Pargiter said if I really want to do Shakespeare I should just do it because that's the new thing now. Women doing the male parts. So you get something truly epic or – whatsit. Tragic. Even with women. She suggested *Hamlet* but Fiona says *Hamlet*'s just a wankfest for boys. Five hours of some twat thinking out loud and then killing himself. Boring.

Neil Bridget.

Bridget What?

Neil You just
  you can't call *Hamlet* boring. It's not boring. It's great art.

Bridget Come on, it is a bit boring.

Neil It's about the human condition.

Bridget Not really.

Neil Course it is.

Bridget But Hamlet's a prince!

Neil Exactly. I think Ophelia's a great idea.

Bridget What?

Neil For your audition.

Bridget I'm not doing Ophelia. I'm going to do a man speech.

Neil Are you?

Bridget I just told you that.

Neil Oh.

Bridget You only listened when I started slagging off *Hamlet*.

Neil I was listening!

Bridget Will you help me learn my lines?

Neil When?

Bridget When I know who I'm going to be.

Neil Ask your sister.

Bridget I'm asking you.

Neil I'd love to it's just I'm up to my eyeballs this week. When's the audition?

Bridget It doesn't matter.

Neil Maybe next week?

Bridget It's OK. I'll ask Alice. It's not like she's doing anything else. Ever.

Neil Huh.

Bridget What time's dinner?

Neil Uh
I'm just doing this then I'll make a start. Maybe in about an hour?

Bridget An hour! Have we got any crisps?

Neil Don't stuff a load of crisps now. You won't be hungry.

Bridget OK I won't.

She gets a massive bag of crisps out of the cupboard. Then:

How did Mum's thing go?

Neil What's that?

Bridget Mum. Her pitch thing. How did it go?

Neil Oh right. Uh. I haven't spoken to her. Well, I have spoken to her but she didn't say.

Bridget Did she say what time she'd be home?

Neil doesn't answer.

After a moment, Bridget shrugs, exits.

Neil taps at his iPad. He chuckles.

After another moment, Alice enters. She is wearing a grubby black-and-white onesie with head and tails (a skunk).

She goes over to the knife rack and takes out a large kitchen knife.

Neil looks up. Watches her. Looks back down at his iPad.

She turns and carries the knife out of the room.

Pause.

Neil laughs.

Then the sound of a key in the door.

The front door opens and slams.

Neil doesn't look up from his iPad.

Neil I'm in here!

A pause.

After a while, Linda enters. Neil doesn't look up.

Linda Did you put the heating on?

Neil Hm?

Linda It's warm in here. Or maybe it's just cold out there. It's autumn all of a sudden.

Neil Have we got any mushrooms?

Linda I don't know. Hello.

Neil Hi.

Linda How was your day?

Neil Ah, you know. The usual.

Linda Where are the girls?

Neil Uh.

Linda Did Alice get up yet?

Neil I haven't seen her.

Linda What time did you get home?

Neil Dunno. 'Bout four? I saw someone.

Linda Someone?

Neil Bridget!

Linda / Was it Bridget?

Neil It was Bridget. She wanted crisps.

Linda Oh that child.

Neil Huh.

Linda Are you marking?

Neil Not right now.

Neil has gone back to his iPad.

Linda watches him for a moment. Then:

Linda So I did my pitch.

Neil Oh yes! How did it go?

Linda Well . . . I don't want to speak too soon but
on the whole
I think I nailed it!

Neil Yes?

Linda I was passionate. I was motivational.

Neil Hurray!

Linda I demanded the return of True Beauty in a new
guise.

Neil Uh-huh.

Linda God, it felt good. It was like the old days. You
know? I'm not just pitching an ad. I'm starting a
revolution!

Neil Super.

Linda All being well, I should be able to pitch it in Munich next month.

Neil Sounds good.

Linda Oh God. The new Brand Strategist. You should have heard her.

Neil Mmm?

Linda She's this incredibly bright young thing Kenina's got in from l'Audace. Gorgeous. She's meant to be a real hot shot. But her presentation was all crow's feet and fine lines and blah blah. Science. Whatever. I felt a bit sorry for her but you know Dave. He's so supportive of young people.

Neil So long as yours went well.

Linda It really did. I mean we should find out on Monday for sure but I might get thinking about artwork. Be good to have something to show the Germans.

Neil Have we got any mushrooms?

Linda I'll have a look.

Neil Thought I might try my hand at a mushroom risotto.

Linda Really?

Neil Found a recipe online.

Linda Uh.
I don't think we have.
No.

Neil Oh.

She opens the fridge.

Linda I can make you a risotto with chicken? Would you like that?

Neil I'm doing it.

Linda That's OK, darling. I don't have time to clean the whole kitchen tonight, I want to get going on some visuals. And anyway haven't you got practice?

Neil We're doing a late one.

Linda How's it going?

Neil Getting ready for this open-mic thing.

He presses something on his laptop, music starts to play.

Linda You still don't want me to come?

Neil Next time.

Linda But it's going well?

Neil Yeah. Stevie's got a cold. Which probably means hungover. But other than that we're getting there. I hope.

Linda I'm so jealous. Honestly.

Neil What?

Linda Not in a bad way.

Neil She's very annoying.

Linda What?

Neil Stevie. She's pretty but her personality
I mean
talk about hard work.

Linda What are you on about?

Neil I know she's young and obviously she's very attractive but you've got no reason to be jealous, Linda.

Beat.

Linda I didn't mean that.

Neil When?

Linda I meant of you. Going off to be in a band. Why would I be jealous of Stevie?

Neil I thought / you said

Linda You think there's some reason I should be jealous?

Neil Not at all.

Linda Then why did you say it?

Neil Because
you said you were jealous! I just thought because I'm spending a lot of time with her and I asked you not to come to the gig.

Linda Right.

Neil Some people might be jealous.

Linda Do you want me to be jealous?

Neil No!

Linda Really?

Neil Maybe because of what you said about work.

Linda What did I say?

Neil About the girl at work.

Bridget enters.

Linda What a funny thing to say! Honestly, Neil.

She does a funny voice:

'Sort It Out!'

Bridget I'm becoming a man!

Linda Say hello to me please.

Bridget Hello, Mum.

Linda Hello, Mum, how was work today? It was good thank you, Bridget. I'm making risotto. Does that sound good?

From this point on, Linda is whipping up an impressive dinner as she talks.

Bridget Can't we have pasta?

Linda I can make you pasta if you want pasta. Would you rather have pasta? Your father's having risotto.

Bridget Pasta please.

Linda Where's your sister? She's not still in bed is she?

Bridget Upstairs. Dunno.

Linda Did she get dressed today?

Bridget What do you think?

Linda Honestly. I despair. I really do. Can you get me the butter out the fridge?
What did you do today, please? Proper details not vague.

Bridget Not much.

Linda How was school?

Bridget Fine. Here you go.

Linda Give me a kiss.
What does fine mean?

Bridget It was fine. I'm going to do a man. For my audition speech for Cynthia Lane.

Linda I thought you were doing Ophelia.

Bridget Everyone does Ophelia. I want to do something different.

Linda Ophelia's a great part. She has that whole thing with the going mad doesn't she?

Bridget Fiona says *Hamlet*'s boring.

Linda Goodness. I'm sure your father has an opinion about that. Don't you, Neil?

Neil What's that?

Linda *Hamlet.*

Bridget A wankfest for boys.

Linda A what?

Neil We've been through this. *Hamlet*'s not 'for boys'. We can all identify with Hamlet. He's universal.

Linda There you go.

Bridget If I do anything from *Hamlet* I'm doing Hamlet. He's got the most lines.

Linda You have to show them what parts you could do in the real world. You can't just turn up in a pair of tracksuit trousers pretending to be a boy. You won't get in.

Alice enters, carrying the knife and some cardboard Amazon packaging. She proceeds to shove the rubbish in the bin and put the knife back in place, as:

Bridget They can't not be impressed if I do Macbeth. Or King Lear. Or who's the other one?

Linda Do Ophelia. We'll get you a nice dress and do your hair.

Alice enters.

Like that painting. Oh look, she's alive! Hi, Mum, how was your day? Fine thank you, Alice. How was yours?

Alice Shit. Who's the other one what?

Bridget Famous king. I'm going to do a man for my audition.

Alice / Why?

Linda Did / you just wake up?

Bridget So Cynthia Lane thinks I'm a / groundbreaking actor.

Alice No. / You're a what?

Bridget Like / Sir Laurence Olivier.

Linda Do you want some tea?

Alice No thanks. / Cynthia Lane is for stage-school brats.

Linda I'm making risotto.

Alice Not Shakespeare. No thanks.

Linda Or pasta?

Alice I only came down to get rid of my rubbish. You could be a Burger King. Wear one of those paper crowns.

Bridget Fuck off.

Alice Just saying.

Bridget You're just jealous because I'm going to be an actor who changes the world. And you're a nobody.

Alice Hmm, let's think of some actors who've changed the world. Oh no, that's right. There aren't any!

Bridget I can think of one.

Alice Go on.

Bridget She's adopted like
    eight children from war-torn countries and she's an ambassador for the UN.

Linda I know!

Bridget As an actress you're in a powerful position to influence global politics. So long as you make it big and famous. Then you can use your fame for good.

Linda She's also incredibly beautiful.

Alice Yeah, exactly.

Bridget What does that mean?

Linda I just mean it helps if you want to be an actress.

Alice She means you're a fat fuck and no one wants to look at you.

Linda No I did not, Alice! Don't say such horrible things to your sister.

Bridget ⎫ Half-sister.
Alice ⎭ Half-sister.

Linda I'm the European Ambassador for Swan Beauty. What about following in my footsteps? I'm making a better world for you girls to grow up in.

Bridget I want to be an actress!

Alice goes to the window.

Linda Changing the world one girl at a time. And next: one fifty-year-old woman at a time! Hollywood is a superficial place, Bridget. To me you're the most beautiful girl in the world but you should still have a back-up plan. Don't let acting pull focus from your school work.

Alice It's dark already.

Bridget Mrs Pargiter says it's better to be a character actress. Then the parts don't dry up when your beauty fades.

Linda You need to try and get into a better sleep pattern by Monday.

Alice Why what's happening on Monday?

Linda Alice! / For God's sake

Alice It's a joke! I'm joking. I haven't forgotten. Jesus.

Bridget Are you going to go in that outfit?

Alice Why not?

Linda I'm going to assume that's also a joke.

Bridget Professional people don't wear onesies.

Alice How would you know?

Bridget That's what she said.

Linda I'm saying yes to a cute little Diane von Fürstenberg crêpe-de-chine jumpsuit but no to that disgusting old thing you've got on. Darling, you're so pretty! Why do you always hide yourself away like this?

Bridget She says if you don't take if off she'll make you.

Alice No she fucking won't. She knows I can't take it off. / You know I can't take it off.

Linda You can't come into my office looking like that.

Alice I'm only / doing work experience.

Linda You're doing work experience! Experience of work. / You don't go to work in a onesie.

Alice You haven't told them who I am. I'm not doing it if / they know who I am.

Linda As agreed I have not told them who you are. I arranged it all with Carol
  she thinks you're the daughter of a friend of a friend. But that doesn't mean you can act how you want. People will know I got you in.

Alice So what?

Linda So you're a reflection on me.

Alice No I'm not.

Linda You're a beautiful talented young woman with the world at your fingertips.

You know Amy's exactly the same age as you. Twenty-five years old and she's just been headhunted!

Alice Who's Amy?

Linda The new Brand Strategist. Here, take this, you can help me stir.

Alice Why can't Bridget help you?

Linda Because I'm asking you.

Alice I don't even want any.

Linda Just take it.

Alice huffs and takes the spoon.

You've been in bed all day.

Alice So?

Linda So the least you can do is lift a finger.

Alice I'm depressed.

Linda And I'm trying to encourage you back into a place of positivity. You've been here for months. Lounging round in that disgusting thing. Refusing to go out the house. You missed the whole summer!

Alice I'm doing your work experience, aren't I?

Linda There's a whole world out there. A beautiful world beyond the dark smelly confines of your bedroom. A world / beyond Xbox

Bridget My bedroom.

Linda and *Doctor Who* DVDs

Alice A world of beauty creams and face-wipes!

Linda Yes! Actually. The Swan offices are such a nurturing
    nourishing environment. The air always smells of a different lotion
    coconut or vanilla or roses
    we have fruit in baskets. Fresh flowers on the tables.
And it's an excellent opportunity to find an actual career.
Swan's full of young women like you. You might
    dare I say it
    make friends.

Alice With 'Amy the Brand Strategist'?

Linda Why not?

Alice I hate the name Amy.

Linda You could learn a lot from someone like Amy.

Alice Like how to be a vapid cunt?

Linda Like
    don't say cunt
    she has wonderful sense of style. Her pitch was awful
but she looked fabulous. Effortless. She'd be a great role
model for you. Since you seem to find me so laughable.

Alice Here we go.

Linda When I was the same age as Bridget I was living
on my own already. / Fending for myself.

Bridget You weren't on your own, you were with Auntie
Barbara.

Linda Auntie Barbara was only a year older than me.
And now look at me. An award-winning businesswoman
and I didn't even go to university. Mother of two.
Gorgeous husband. I can change a tyre, I own my own
home, dinner-party guests marvel at my home-made

croqembouche and I still fit into the same size-ten dress
suit I did fifteen years ago. I've washed
   brushed
   groomed
   plucked
   shaved
   painted
   injected
   dyed
   dieted
   oh God I've dieted. My whole life I've been watching
what I eat and watching what I say and watching how
I walk
   how I talk
   what I wear. Because that's what you have to do when
you're a woman, girls. We do what they do only
backwards and in heels. And all this while achieving.
Climbing. Raising children. You feel guilty at work cos
you're not with your kids. You feel guilty at home cos
you're not at work. But I've done it. By God, Linda
Wilde has done it. I've made it to the top and believe me
   if I can do it
   you can do it. If you're prepared to do the work?
   You really can have it all.

Alice Is this what you say to the kids in your low self-
esteem workshops?

Linda Well. Building up self-esteem is about making
people realise the power of their full potential. The only
thing standing in your way is yourself. You see?

Alice Unless there's something actually holding you back
like racism or sexism.

Linda Those things can't hold you back. You've got to
think positive, Alice. The mind is an incredibly powerful
tool.

Alice OK Mum.

Linda Don't take sexist or racist people too seriously. Don't give stupid people too much importance.

Alice Don't take them seriously?

Linda Honestly, Alice. You've got no reason not to be the most confident girl on the planet. Most girls would kill to look like you.

Alice No reason?

Linda No reason at all!

Alice Are you fucking JOKING?

Alice throws the spoon down and storms out.

Linda What did I say? Alice! Don't be like that!

Neil What happened? What was that about?

Linda I don't know. Bridget, what happened?

Bridget She's a bitch. That's what happened.

Linda Don't call your sister a bitch.

Bridget Well, she is a bitch.

Linda I'm not trying to pressure her. But she could at least let me put that thing in the washing machine.

Bridget She thinks it's magical. Some kind of a talisman.

Linda What?

Bridget She says if she takes it off something bad will happen.

Linda Does she?

Neil Oh come on. She knows she'll never get a job as long as she's wearing it and she'll do whatever it takes not to get a job. We should start charging her rent. / She'd drop all this depressed nonsense quick enough after that. Mark my words.

Linda Please don't start on the rent thing again, Neil, I've told you I'm not charging her rent there's no point she's got no money.

Neil You're enabling her. Sometimes people have to hit rock bottom before they climb their way back up. You know that. You bought her a new iPhone, for God's sake!

Bridget I want a new iPhone.

Linda You don't need a new iPhone.

Bridget You said if you got your bonus I could get a new iPhone.

Linda Oh thank you, Bridget. I so enjoy being reminded that I didn't get my bonus. What's your point?

Bridget What about a new Samsung?

Linda No!

Bridget And she's living in my bedroom. I don't even have my own bedroom any more.

Linda Did I ask Neil to turn her bedroom into a recording studio?

Neil She's twenty-five years old. People are married by that age. They have kids.

Linda Not many people these days. The problem is they don't realise what an advantage they've got. My God, if I'd had half the opportunities you girls have? I'd be running the world. These are the years you mustn't waste. You want to be a success? You've got to start young.

Neil has put his headphones in.

There's no time to lose!

FOUR

Girls' bedroom. It's a temporary-looking arrangement.

Alice is in bed. Wearing her onesie.
    Bridget is getting undressed.
    She takes off her clothes as though she's in public, hiding any possible nudity.

Alice Get into bed I want to turn the light out.

Bridget Hang on.

Alice Just take your fucking clothes off. I'm not looking.

Bridget Yes you are.

Alice No one wants to look at your disgusting body OK?

    Beat.

Bridget Why do you hate me so much?

Alice I don't hate you, you're just incredibly annoying.

Bridget Mum says it's hard for you because for a long time there was just you and you got all the attention and then one day I came along and you had to share it with me.

Alice Mum's an idiot. I never got all the attention. Her work did. She palmed me off on babysitters most of the time.

Bridget Is that why you hate her?

Alice No. I hate her because she's a fake.

Bridget No she's not.

Alice All she cares about is what other people think.

Bridget If that's true why did she go to my parents' evening in that hat?

Alice That ridiculous hat. Why do you think? For attention! She does everything for attention. She's mental.

Bridget Like mother like daughter. Some people might say you wear that onesie all the time for attention.

Alice Hardly.

Bridget 'Look at me. I'm a kitten!'

Alice I'm not a kitten, I'm a skunk, you fool. And this onesie means the opposite. It's my camouflage. It means don't look at me.

Bridget That's what everyone says about Gemma Pascoe. Oh she wants to be invisible that's why she stopped eating. She wants to be so thin she vanishes but actually
   since she stopped eating
   she's had loads of attention from everyone *and* her dad came over from Australia to visit her.

Alice What are you on about?

Bridget If she really wanted people to stop noticing her she'd be like me and eat normally and be boring. See?

Alice You're not boring, you're just
   average. There's nothing wrong with that.

Bridget I don't want to be average.

Alice It's better to be average. Trust me. At your age there's nothing worse than standing out from the crowd.

Bridget Like you did?

Alice You're lucky you get to learn from my mistakes.

Bridget How come you don't just get a job?

Alice I had a job.

Bridget But you didn't like it?

Alice I don't like life.

Bridget Maybe you need a goal.

Alice I've got a goal.

Bridget What's your goal?

Alice To wear my onesie till I die.

Bridget Hm.

Alice Don't judge my goal.

Bridget I'm not, I just think
maybe you need to blog about it. You know if people knew that was your goal and they could like
tune into a YouTube video of you wearing your onesie for example in funny places

Alice I don't want to do that

Bridget no I'm just saying that might make it a better goal. You might get a book deal.

Alice What did I just say? I don't want to be famous. I've been famous. It's shit. It made me want to kill myself.

Bridget gasps.

Bridget You can't say that!

Alice Why not?

Bridget Because of Granny Wilde.

Alice Oh my God, Bridget. Shut up. I can say what I want. And you can't call someone 'Granny' who you never met. OK? Why are you such a twat?

Bridget I'm not the one claiming to be famous.

Alice You know what I mean. Dick. Get into bed.

Bridget gets into bed.

They lie there for a bit.

Bridget I don't want to be average. I want to get bitten by a vampire and turn into a vampire and go round sucking virgins' blood and live forever.

Alice Realistic.

Bridget I want to live in a squat and inject heroin. And
I want to be attacked by a shark
or wolves
and have impressive scars on my torso that only a man who loves me will ever get to see. And
I want my emails to be published after I'm dead. And I want to get shipwrecked on a desert island with an explorer who falls passionately in love with me and when we finally get rescued he takes me to live in his Victorian town house
full of books
where he dies
leaving me alone with a hundred stray cats.

Alice You read too much.

Bridget I want to go to Nashville and have a lesbian affair with a country-and-western singer who betrays her Christian beliefs to be with me. And
I want to get sentenced to five years in prison for armed robbery, but get off on a technicality and end up only spending six months inside. And
I want to kill a baddie and be hailed as a hero. And I want to eat monkey brains and shop in a souk and go on the run so I have to dye my hair in a petrol station toilet. And

Alice You know what I want?

Bridget Go on.

Alice I want you to shut the fuck up and turn the light out.

Bridget looks at her. Scowls.

Turns out the light.

A pause.

Bridget Alice?

Alice What?

Bridget Are you asleep?

Alice Obviously not.

   Beat.

What?

Bridget I'm sorry about what happened. When you were at school.

Alice Shut up. Go to sleep.

FIVE

Dave's office.
   Dave, Amy and Linda are having a meeting.
   There is a long pause. Eventually:

Dave Linda?

Linda I'm sorry I just
   I'm feeling confused.

Dave I don't think it's complicated.

Linda It's not complicated it's just
   I'm struggling to take it in.

Dave I don't know how many more times I can say it, Linda. We didn't ask for True Beauty. We don't want True Beauty. How can that
   are you honestly telling me you're surprised?

39

Linda But it's such an innovative idea. I thought you'd be excited.

Dave Did you not hear the stats Amy presented? Where are they? I wrote them down somewhere, ah here we go. Ageing is the number one beauty concern for six out of ten women over the age of twenty-seven. The number one
    beauty concern. Six out of ten women.

He looks at Linda.

It's the number one beauty concern for eight out of ten women over the age of thirty-four. Number one concern! Eight out of ten!

Linda Didn't you also say it was the number one concern for ten out of ten women over the age of fifty?

Dave Linda, your idea ignored a huge section of the potential market. Why target the over-fifties when we can also sell this product to women in their forties? Thirties? Twenties!

Linda But my idea

Dave The bottom line is

Linda I just feel like

Dave Stop! Linda! Just
    stop for a minute OK? Calm down. Listen to me: listen. We hired Amy to be a fresh voice. To inject some new energy. And that's what she's doing. Maybe we could all try and take a leaf out of her book. Yes?

Linda I'm sorry I'm just
    I wasn't expecting this.

Dave I find that very hard to imagine but. OK.

Beat.

Linda Sorry.

Amy Not at all.

Linda Congratulations.

Amy Thank you, Linda.

Beat.

Dave Change is necessary. Right?

Linda I mean

Dave The Swan woman has evolved. Yes it was nice
    for a while
    to be told to embrace her chubby thighs and frizzy hair
and to love her freckles but it's like Amy says
    as a brand
    the ultimate result of that campaign was that we
stopped being aspirational.

Linda I / just think

Dave Anyway, anyway. Look.
    I don't want you to worry too much, Linda, OK? I
think it's better we let Amy handle it since it's her baby.
Sit back. Let the youngsters do the hard work for a
change. Yes?

Amy Fine with me.

Linda Sit back?

Dave Let's just give Amy a chance to get stuck in with
her 'Hi-Beautiful' idea shall we, Linda? Share some of
your amazing wisdoms with her? Support. Advise.
Answer any questions she might have. Then you can just
    put your feet up!

SIX

Linda's office.

Alice and Luke.
   She is wearing office clothes over her onesie. You can tell if you know, but not otherwise.
   Luke is doing some filing.

Luke There's a big store cupboard up on eight? Stacked full of freebies. You can go in and help yourself? If you're into that kind of thing.

Alice Are you not?

Luke I'm a temp. I just got sent here through the agency.

Alice Ah.

Luke I'm saving up. I want to be on my way to Bali by the end of the month. I was doing construction stuff before this but my mate Kayley was like
   go work in an office, Luke. You get paid just as much and you do fuck-all?

Alice You're going to Bali?

Luke The only downside is you have to listen to the beauty chat. I'm like, jeez people. Do you guys not recognise a negative data stream when you hear it?

Alice A what?

Luke Have you met Linda yet?

Alice Uh. I think so.

Luke She's a character.

Alice Is she?

Luke She fucking loves me. Watch her flirt with me. You'll see.

Alice Oh.

Luke Amy bet me five hundred quid I couldn't get her to shag me. She's so twisted.

Alice Who?

Luke Amy.

Alice Linda flirts with you?

Luke It's pretty full-on.

Alice Isn't she married?

Luke Yeah, I'd never do it. I've actually quit sex? Well. Not technically but I'm thinking about it cos like
   semen contains extraordinary amounts of energy? So I'd rather keep it in?

Alice How come you're going to Bali?

Luke Oh. Right. I'm going to this camp with these people who all think the same as I do? We're called the Free Thinkers. We're into this thing called the Big Wisdom? Have you heard of it?

Alice I don't think so.

Luke I can lend you a book if you like.

Alice Maybe. What is it you believe?

Luke We don't believe. Belief implies faith. We 'think'. We think there's no such thing as reality? This table. This filing cabinet. You. It's all an illusion.

Alice OK.

Luke I'm talking about a group of people who are enlightened.

Alice In Bali?

Luke We're all over the planet but we've got a centre in

Bali. And one near Brixton. But I want to go to Bali and do the training to become a trainer to train others.

Alice Train others in what?

Luke In how to be enlightened. The world would be a much better place if instead of fighting wars and killing each other we all just sat back

took a deep breath

and tried to focus on the essential truth that all we have is now

and it's all an illusion.

Alice I think

Luke We need to cease the endless desire to chase or change data? We're all part of the material of the cosmos. Who we are right now? In this moment? We are perfect.

Beat.

Alice I like that.

Luke It's the truth.

Alice Huh.

The door opens and Linda enters.

Linda Ah. Alice. You're here.

Alice I'm just helping Luke / with the filing.

Linda No, that's great, I just wanted to make sure you're being looked after. I'm going to plough through some emails then I think I might head home early. I don't feel very well. You've got things to do?

Alice I think so. Are you OK?

Linda Luke's looking after you?

Alice He is.

Linda Thanks, Luke. You're a star. Did you bring the post in?

Luke Shit. / Sorry.

Linda It's OK. If you can get it asap that would be lovely.

Luke Sure, hun.

Linda Thanks.

Luke No worries.

Luke exits, grinning at Alice on his way.

Linda shuts the door.

She turns and hurries to the mirror.

Alice What's wrong?

Linda I think I've got a migraine coming on.

Alice You shouldn't flirt with him, it's inappropriate.

Linda Who?

Alice Who do you think?

Linda isn't listening.

What did Dave say?

Linda About what?

Alice I thought you had a meeting with Dave about your pitch.

Linda Oh right. I did. He uh
didn't go for it.

Beat.

Alice Sorry to hear that.

Linda Turn round. Let me look at you.

Alice It looks fine. It looks like tights.

Linda And no one's said anything?

Alice You can't tell!

Linda Maybe today you can't tell. What about when you wear that every day?

Alice I'll work out new ways to cover it up.

Linda Alice

Alice It's fine. Don't stress. Seriously. I'm having a good time.

Linda You are?

Alice It's OK. Yeah.

Linda I'm so pleased!

Alice I said it's 'OK'. Don't go mad.

Linda Did you go down to HR and introduce yourself?

Alice Not yet.

Linda Floor six. Speak to Carol. Is Luke showing you the ropes?

Alice Yeah, he seems nice.

Linda And he's 'not bad looking' either!

Alice Mum!

Linda You could do a lot worse!

There is a knock at the door.

Alice Shut up.

Linda Come in!

As the door opens, Alice turns away to shove the last bit of filing away. Amy enters.

Amy. Hi.

Amy Hey Linda. How's it going? Can we have a quick word?

Alice turns round. She stares at Amy.

Linda Sure.

Amy looks at Alice.

Oh uh. Amy this is Alice. She's here on work experience.

Amy Hi. Great to meet you.

Alice Hi.

Amy I love your shoes. Are they vintage?

Alice I think they're just
old.

Amy Awesome.

Beat.

Um. So I just wanted a little catch-up?

Alice I'll leave you to it.

Linda Thanks, Alice.

Amy Nice to meet you.

Alice looks at Amy.

Then exits.

Beat.

Amy wanders over to the window.

I love the view from your window. Look at that. Over the river. The bridge. Best office in the building.

Linda It's beautiful, isn't it?

Amy Lucky you're not scared of heights. I'd be terrified.

Linda Oh no. I love it up here.

Amy God, Linda I feel so terrible about this.

Linda About . . . ?

Amy That meeting was so awkward. I don't know why Dave chose to tell us like that. You know?

   Beat.

So I just wanted to come in and talk to you face to face and make sure there's no bad blood between us. Because
   obviously it's unusual. I arrive one minute and then next minute I'm kind of telling you what to do and stuff. So I wanted to let you know how much I admire you. You've been a real role model for me. You know?

Linda OK.

Amy True Beauty pretty much inspired me to go into this industry. So. And I'm literally going to feel completely crazy about being in charge of you so I just want you to feel able to come to me with anything
   anything at all you're worried about or you disagree with? Because I massively respect your opinion. Please don't think I won't listen. My door isn't just open to you it's like

   Amy gestures with her arms wide.

   Beat.

I will honour your legacy. I promise.

Linda My legacy?

Amy Is that the wrong word?

Linda I don't know.

Amy And just to reassure you about Hi-Beautiful? As a twenty-five-year-old woman? I would totally buy this product. I'm serious. Some of my friends are getting botox already. It's not like you have to be fifty to worry about getting old. I'm like

oh shit I thought I'd be married by now. I thought I'd own a house by now. You know?

Linda I see.

Amy I am engaged. But I mean I have nightmares about hitting thirty!

Amy laughs.

Linda doesn't laugh.

Amy stops laughing.

Beat.

Oh. Was that insensitive?

Linda Don't be silly.

Amy I'm such a blonde sometimes. I didn't mean to offend you.

Linda You didn't offend me.

Amy Phew.

Linda Thanks for coming by.

Amy No, thank you for listening!

Beat.

Fab, well I'll leave you to it I'm sure you're very busy so. I'm really happy we had this chat. And I'm just

I'm over the moon to be working with you. I can't wait to get started.

Amy heads out. Then stops.

Oh! Actually do you think you've got time to do another PowerPoint? Dave wants us to announce the new direction company-wide, I thought it might be nice for you to get up and introduce the basic premise before I do the big presentation? Can I leave that with you?

Linda I mean

Amy Awesome. Thanks, Linda.

Linda Thanks, Amy.

Amy leaves. Linda stands for a moment. She presses her hand to her head.

SEVEN

Spotlight on Stevie, standing at a mic. She's singing:

Stevie Tick tock tick tock tick tock tick tock –

It's Gwen Stefani, 'What You Waiting For?'

But when it's time for the first verse, she loses her words.

The music carries on for a bit.

Fuck! I can't remember how it goes. Sorry. Can we start again?

EIGHT

Dave's office.

Linda has come to talk to Dave.

Dave No, I'm sorry, Linda you've lost me.

Linda I think we need to go back to the groups. We can't just go full steam ahead before we know how our customers will respond. / We're a trusted brand.

Dave This is way past the group stage, Linda. You know that.

Linda If you ask me, Dave, I think it's very dangerous / to assume

Dave I didn't / ask you.

Linda that our customers
    what?

Dave I said I didn't ask you, Linda. What I asked you was for your support. I asked you to be supportive.

Linda I am supportive, of course I'm supportive / I just

Dave This doesn't feel very supportive.

Linda I think you're making a mistake.

Dave Uh-huh?

Linda As Senior Brand Manager I need to make it clear that I object to Amy's idea. I'm not only disappointed you didn't choose Visibility but moreover I think Hi-Beautiful could be / catastrophic for us.

Dave It's OK, Linda. It's OK for you to object. And I don't feel I need to know the reasons why. You're allowed to feel whatever you want.

Linda It contradicts everything we stand for!

Dave I'm sorry, but I'm getting sick of repeating myself. We all know how much True Beauty meant to you, Linda –

Linda Changing the world one girl at a time.

Dave And there we go, she said the slogan! Can we please leave True Beauty behind, Linda? Can we do that?

Linda What about 'Reflections of my Mother'? People wept when they saw that advert! They went home and told their daughters they were beautiful no matter what!

Dave We don't want people to weep. We want them to buy!

Linda We want them to change the way they feel about themselves!

Dave Only if it makes them buy!

Linda I can't believe I'm hearing this!

Dave Look. I've made my decision. You had your chance to pitch your idea. We listened. We deliberated. But I've got to tell you
    this was the worst one yet, OK? It came across as some kind of
    bizarre
    drum-banging. Now obviously this stuff is sensitive for you. I understand that. It's partly why I decided to pass the cream over to Amy. Someone who might be more – objective. About getting older. Because it's a touchy subject. I can see you're very agitated about it.

Linda Getting older?

Dave But personal
    paranoia
    is not the basis and should not be the basis of a marketing campaign. We all want what's best for Swan, right? Yes, we're changing direction. And I understand why you're apprehensive. We all are. I know Amy's petrified! But she's also talented and brilliant and I believe she can lead this. Don't you?

Linda This isn't about Amy.

Dave I'm giving her the same opportunity I gave you back in the day. When you were just starting out.

Linda Back in the day there was no Senior Brand Manager. Now there is!

Dave OK, Linda now listen. You don't work in this industry as long as I have and not get to know a little bit about women. Right? I know what you girls are like. I know Amy's young. And obviously she's very attractive. But I'm asking you to please

please be a team player on this one, OK, Linda? Try not to feel threatened by Amy.

Linda Threatened? Dave. I'm an award-winning business woman. I'm happily married with two beautiful daughters and I still fit in the same size-ten dress suit I did fifteen years ago. What could possibly threaten me?

NINE

Home. Afternoon.

Linda stands very still.
  Stevie is here, just wearing one of Neil's T-shirts and her knickers.

Linda I wasn't feeling well. I came home early.

Stevie Right.

Linda It's a school day. He should be at school.

Stevie He called in sick.

Linda Oh.

Stevie He said you wouldn't be back.

Linda No, well, I wasn't meant to be. I've got a pain in my head. It won't go away.

Stevie OK.

  Beat.

Linda It suits you. That T-shirt.

Beat.

I got him that online. Doesn't fit him very well. Bit small. Do you shop online? Apart from the fact that half the stuff you get doesn't fit it's so convenient isn't it? Saves you trudging round the shops I find. The only thing is waiting for it to arrive in the post and never quite knowing if it's going to get through the letterbox or if you'll have to go to the depot and pick the bloody thing up at which point really well you might just as well have gone to the shops. Unless it's coming from abroad. If it's coming from abroad then of course it's more convenient but then it can take an awfully long time to arrive can't it? And one time I ordered a dressing gown and it turned out it was coming from China and when it arrived there was a sodding customs charge!

Beat.

So apart from things being the wrong size and going to the post office instead of your house and taking months to arrive and costing extra it's really very
very convenient.

Beat.

I think I need to sit down.

Stevie Sorry.

Linda No it's fine I just
my head . . .

Linda sits.

Stevie stands awkwardly.

Pause.

Stevie tugs at the bottom of the T-shirt.

Stevie I was just getting a glass of water.

Linda Thirsty?

Stevie I am a bit.

Linda Can be dehydrating, can't it?

Beat.

When I first met Neil
    God, we used to fuck like rabbits.

Linda laughs.

Probably goes down on you and everything, does he? I remember those days. Although to be fair that was never Neil's strong point. He used to go at it like a pig in a trough. What's he doing up there?

Stevie Taking a shower.

Linda Taking a shower. Of course.

Linda giggles.

What's he going to do now?

Stevie I don't know.

Beat.

Shall I get him?

Linda Maybe. I feel strangely nervous at the thought of seeing him. But I suppose it would be awfully weird for us just to pretend this never happened, wouldn't it? You'd be caught in a world of secrets. You might run mad.

Stevie I'll get him.

Linda Drown yourself.

Stevie What?

Linda I'm in shock. Maybe. Do you think I'm in shock?

Beat.

Stevie I didn't
   mean for any of this to happen and I know there's
nothing I can say to make it better but I am genuinely
   so
   so
   sorry.

Linda Thank you.

Stevie I don't know your name.

Linda He didn't tell you my name?

   Beat.

My name is Linda.

   Beat.

Stevie I'm going to go and get Neil now. OK?

Linda OK.

   Stevie goes to the door. Hesitates.

Stevie I know this probably doesn't help at all but
   he doesn't love me.

Linda How do you know?

Stevie He just
   I don't know. I feel like if someone is in love with you
they should like
   want to know everything about you. You know? Like
   what you were like at school or what your middle
name is or if you've got a best friend. But Neil always
says he likes me being a mystery. He says it's better that
way.

Linda Neil said that?

   Stevie nods.

How odd.

Stevie Well.

So . . .

I just wanted to tell you that.

TEN

Open-plan office space.

Amy and Luke.

Amy She actually quoted the old slogan. Can you believe that? He's told her fifty billion times to drop it but she just can't let it go.

Luke Dave told you this?

Amy She went in and tried to persuade him to drop my campaign. Thankfully Dave's got my back so he told her to go fuck herself. At which point she decided she had such a terrible headache she had to go home. So much for sisterhood, eh?

Luke Sounds to me like she spoke her truth.

Amy She won a couple of awards like literally ten years ago! Why does she have to be so insanio?

Alice enters.

When are you going to do your bet?

Luke I'm gonna do it. You watch. She adores me.

Amy I'll believe it when I see it.

Alice's presence makes them shift. Move on.

Luke You want to see it?

Amy Fuck off.

57

Luke Hi babe.

Amy What time is it? I've got a catch-up with Kenina.

Luke Just gone two. I'd better get the post in. I've got your book by the way.

Alice My what?

Luke That book you wanted to borrow.

Alice Oh.

Luke Hang on –

Amy Uh-oh. Watch yourself. He's trying to brainwash you!

Luke I'm trying to set her free. Here you go.

Alice *The Big Wisdom. Set Yourself Free.*

Luke See?

Alice Cool.

Amy Insanio!

Luke Insanio!

Amy Insanio!

 They laugh.

Luke Give me a shout if you need anything else, babe, yeah?

Alice Thanks.

Luke I'll be back in a sec. See you later, Ames.

Amy See ya!

 He goes.

 She laughs. Looks at Alice. Alice doesn't smile. Amy turns.

I better go.

She starts getting her papers together. Her phone. She's going to leave but she notices Alice is still standing there, staring at her.

Do you need something, hun?

Alice No.

Beat.

Amy How are you finding it? Are we all a bit mad?

Alice It's OK.

Amy How you getting on with Linda?

Alice Fine.

Amy How many times has she mentioned her award?

Alice I don't know. None I don't think.

Amy Don't worry. She will. Me and Luke are counting. When we get to a hundred we're going to go the pub and have a bottle of champagne.

Alice She seems OK to me.

Amy Yeah I thought she was OK at first. Then she started hating my fucking guts.

Alice Why?

Amy Why do you think? You know what it's like. Or you'll see anyway. Predominantly female environments like this are so fucking bitchy? And Linda's insanely menopausal you literally never know where you stand.

Alice I mean

Amy It's OK, she's gone home. She's 'got a headache'.

Amy pulls a face. Then laughs.

Beat.

Luke's cool though, right?

Alice He seems OK.

Amy I see he's got you involved in his crazy religion already.

Alice I'm just reading the book.

Amy Did he tell you he's saving up to go travelling?

Alice Yeah.

Amy Did he tell you he fakes his timesheet every week and Linda doesn't even notice?

Alice No.

Amy It's hilarious. He's basically on double pay.

Alice Really?

Amy Don't tell anyone! He'd get fired.

Alice You don't / remember me, do you?

Amy Linda would flip her lid.
    How do you mean?

Alice You're Amy Harper. You went to St Saviour's.

Amy Yes?

  Beat.

Alice I'm Alice Collier.

Amy No you're not.

  Beat.

Oh my
    God!
    You are, aren't you? Oh my God!
    Alice!
    Fuck!

Alice You didn't recognise me.

Amy What are you doing here?

Alice Work experience.

Amy Work experience?

Beat.

That's
   fantastic!
   God!
   Talk about a small world. Look at you! I didn't recognise you without the

She waves her hands round her head.

you've cut all your hair off!

Beat.

Alice Yeah.

Amy I can't believe you recognised me. I look so different.

Alice Not really.

Amy No, I do. I was such an ugly duckling.

Beat.

How are you? What have you been doing since school?

Alice Not a lot.

Beat.

Amy Last I heard you were working for the council. Somewhere weird.

Alice Plymouth.

Amy That's it. How d'you end up there?

Alice It's where I went to uni.

Amy Didn't you want to be a doctor?

Alice No.

Amy No?
Oh.
Maybe I remembered it wrong.

Beat.

Did you know I'm getting married?

Alice No.

Amy He's a barrister.
So.

Beat.

Are you seeing anyone?

Alice No.

Amy You still in touch with Damon or

Alice Damon?

Amy I just wondered if you'd kept in touch. / You two were inseparable.

Alice Is that meant to be funny? No. I didn't keep in touch with Damon.

Amy I bet he'd love to hear from you. You know he's married now. He's got a kid. Can you believe that?

At this moment Luke comes back in with the post. Starts handing it out round the office.

Luke Ladies. The post has arrived. Better late than never, eh?

Beat.

Amy Hi.

They look at him. Then back at each other.

Alice I'm meant to sign some papers down in HR. I should go.

Amy Oh, OK. Yeah, I should get on but hey, listen, it's so great to see you. We should have a drink before you leave, yeah? Maybe Friday or something?

Alice Maybe.

Amy See you around?

Alice Maybe.

Alice leaves.

Luke, still delivering letters, notices Amy standing, shocked.

Luke She seems nice, eh?

Amy doesn't answer.

Amy?

Amy She went to my school.

Luke Oh.

Amy She used to be so beautiful. I didn't recognise her.

Luke Were you mates?

Amy We were. Then something kind of happened. I shouldn't really say.

Beat.

Do you promise not to tell anyone?

Luke OK.

Amy She got this boyfriend. He kind of put these photos of her online. Like – before that was normal, you know? Before Facebook or anything. I mean, bad photos. Yeah? Graphic.

Luke Oh shit.

Amy Everyone saw them. Literally the whole school. She was infamous. Then next thing you knew, she just – disappeared.

ELEVEN

Home. Afternoon.

Neil sits at the table, staring at his hands.
  Linda, looking a little wild, is staring out of the window.

Neil The first thing I want to say is

Linda I need a drink.

Neil It's three o'clock in the afternoon.

Linda It's three o'clock in the afternoon and I need a fucking drink.

Neil Fine.

Linda My head hurts.

  She takes a glass out of a cupboard.

You want one?

Neil OK.

  She takes another glass out.

  Takes a bottle of whisky out of the lower cupboard.

  Slugs some in the first glass. Hands it to him.

Neil Thanks.

  She slugs some in the second glass. Drinks some. Adds more.

Then slams the bottle down, picks up the glass, and goes to the window.

Pause.

Linda The first thing you want to say is . . . ?

Neil Are you going to sit down?

Linda I'm going to look out the window. If that's OK with you?

Neil Sure.

Beat.

It's windy today.

Linda Indeed.

Neil They're talking about a hurricane.

Linda Are we chatting about the weather?

Neil Right. Sorry.

Beat.

The first thing I want to say is that I'm not going to belittle you or or or disrespect you by lying to you or by being dishonest.

Linda chuckles. Swigs at her drink.

Neil takes a deep breath.

Any more than I already have, obviously.

He clears his throat.

The second thing I want to say is that it was an insane
    madness, Linda. I can't explain it
    I can't
    all I know is when she came upstairs and told me you
were down here I knew like a like a like a like a like a
like an arrow

in my heart
that I love you. That I need you. That I don't want to
lose you. That it was just a silly
meaningless
She fell for me and she's
well you saw her and I just
I've been feeling a bit
and maybe being in the band went to my head. When
she told me she was attracted to me I felt like
all those years as a teenage boy
dreaming of the day I'd be a rock star and pretty girls
would throw
themselves at me and it just seemed so
unfair
that it was happening now. When it was too late.
When it felt too late and then some nasty little thought
came into my head saying
what if it's not too late? You know? What if
what if I can just do it a few times and no one will ever
find out? Because maybe despite my boring old
middle-aged husband and father
schoolteacher exterior
perhaps as it turns out I really am
a rock star. God it sounds pathetic. I know it's
pathetic. I know it is.

Linda presses her fingers to her forehead.

I don't know how it happened. I thought I was better
than this and I tried so hard to be better than this but
I don't know. It turns out I'm just like the worst kind
of wanker and all I can say is it's not what I want. I don't
want her. I don't love her. I love you.

He watches her for a moment. She doesn't respond.

And however you feel right now
whatever it might seem like I can promise you this:

I'm still me! I'm Neil! I'm your Neil! I couldn't
I didn't know what to do.
I made a terrible
terrible mistake. But please
please give me a chance to make it right. I need you.
We're a family. We need to stay together Linda please.
I'm begging you. I'm fucking
Oh God

Neil starts to cry.

Please
please

Linda Bridget will be home soon.

Beat.

Neil Linda?

Linda 'I used to be the protagonist of my life . . .'

Neil What?

Linda You know the funny thing?
When I saw her?
When I saw that girl standing here
in this kitchen
my kitchen I spent months planning and designing and
decorating. The kitchen I spent months doing overtime to
pay for. The kitchen I've cooked your dinner in for more
than a decade. And made your coffee. And poured your
cereal. And cleaned and cleaned and
when I saw that girl standing in my kitchen
wearing your T-shirt
I thought
I knew this would happen.

Neil I didn't plan to do it / I swear to you.

Linda I sat here

waiting for you to come downstairs
and I heard you arguing with her. I heard her start to cry. I heard you get angry. I heard her saying sorry. And I heard you order her to leave.

Neil She's never coming back.

Linda And there was this voice in my head
I couldn't stop it
I think it was my father's voice actually strangely enough I heard my father's voice in my head telling me:
you do know, Linda, don't you – that this is your own fault. When your husband fucks another woman, you've only got yourself to blame.

Neil No!

Linda He doesn't want you any more. And why should he? You're old now, Linda. Your body isn't what it used to be.

Neil Linda, stop! / It's nothing you did.

Linda And you came in here with your hair wet from the shower
your face all flushed and funny looking and I thought my God look at him
what on earth did I ever love about him?

Neil Don't say things like that.

Linda You know what I think it was?

Neil Linda

Linda I wanted to be a woman with a husband.

Neil You're feeling very angry.

Linda But now I'm a woman with a cheating husband.

Neil Don't / make this about more than it is.

Linda I don't want to be a woman with a cheating husband. That doesn't make me feel good. I don't want to be that woman.

Neil This is a blip. This is not about our whole marriage. We're good together. You know we are.

Linda I don't think you love me, Neil. Not really.

Neil I do love you Linda. / I love you more than you know.

Linda I think when someone's in love they should want to know everything about the other person. I think they should be hungry for all the details. Where I went to school. What my middle name is. Whether or not I've got a best friend.

Neil What are you talking about?

Linda Every year I send you an email reminder that my birthday's coming up. And the reason I do that is because I know deep down if I don't do it
    you won't remember and your not remembering will be so painful, Neil
    it will be so painful I won't be able to bear it. So I remind you. I remind you so you don't forget.

Neil April seventeenth.

Linda You've missed the point.

Neil You won't ever have to remind me again. I swear to you.

Linda You're right. I won't need to.

Neil What does that mean?

She turns to him.

Linda? What do you mean?

Linda I want you to go.

Beat.

Neil Where would I go?

Linda I don't care. Somewhere else. Somewhere away from me.

Neil For how long?

Linda For ever.

Neil Linda –

Linda Go! Go on! Get out!

He backs away but keeps trying.

Neil What about Bridget?

Linda What about Bridget?

Neil What if I miss her big audition?

Linda I tell you what. I won't tell her you've gone. Let's see how long it takes her to notice. In fact why don't we get a a a dummy or mannequin or puppet
and sit it at the head of the table and give it an iPad
and we'll see if anyone notices the fucking difference shall we? because
I do everything in this house and the reason I do everything is because I thought at the very least
you were loyal. And reliable. And as it turns out you're not. So now I look at you and I see you for what you are: you're an ornament.

Neil Please

Linda I want you to go upstairs and pack your bags and get out of my house so I can go back. Go back to being someone I want to be!

Neil No –

Linda GET OUT OF MY HOUSE!

TWELVE

Home. Evening.

Bridget is washing up.
    Alice has just got home. She's holding her book.
Wearing her coat, etc.

From upstairs the faint sound of power ballads.

Bridget To be, or not to be!
    That is the question! Whether 'tis better to do *Hamlet*?
or something else.
    What do you think?

Alice Where's Mum?

Bridget I'm running out of time.

Alice I need to talk to her.

Bridget I don't think it's a good time.

Alice I don't care what you think. Where is she?

Bridget First she cleaned all the floors with a toothbrush.
Then she went out. Then she came back and accidentally
broke Dad's big flowerpot. And now she's listening to
shit music and reorganising her wardrobe.

Alice She's listening to music?

Bridget I know.

Alice She never listens to music.

Bridget I think she's upset.

Alice Oh right. Cos Dave didn't choose her stupid idea.

Bridget Is that what happened?

Alice Yeah, he went with another stupid idea instead.

Bridget Poor Mum.

Alice Oh whatever. She'll get over it.

Bridget It's really important to her. You're not going to have a go at her, are you?

Alice Mind your own business. I'll do what I want.

Linda enters, with a magazine.

Linda How is it possible to have an entire wardrobe full of outfits but not a single one of them looks any good on? What are you doing? Why are you doing the washing-up?

Bridget I'm being helpful.

Linda See, this is the thing that pisses me off. Why can't you just say: because the dishes are dirty? You're not *helping me*. It's not *my job* to wash up! It's not all on me! If you girls took any responsibility for anything maybe you'd do the washing-up more often instead of doing it once in a blue moon because you suddenly feel like it.

Alice What are you doing?

Linda I'm looking for something to use as an ashtray.

Bridget You're what?

Linda You heard.

Alice You don't smoke.

Linda Actually that's not true. I used to smoke. I gave up. I gave up because I was pregnant with you. Now I've decided to take it up again.

Bridget You can't!

Linda Why not?

Bridget Because it kills you!

Linda Only if nothing else kills you first.

Bridget You're being weird. What's the matter with you?

Linda I'm having an extremely bad day. Ah. This'll do.

Alice Can I have a cigarette?

Linda If you have one she'll want one.

Bridget Can I have a cigarette?

Linda No! I bought them for me. You can passively smoke mine.

Alice I never knew you smoked.

Linda You don't know a lot of things. I have a whole entire existence and identity of which you are entirely unaware.

Alice Meaning?

Linda Meaning I'm not just your mother.

Alice You smell like booze.

Linda Do I?

Alice and Bridget watch Linda in horror/shock/awe as Linda lights and inhales a cigarette.

Beat.

Bridget Who are you?

Beat.

Linda Oh God.
That's better.
You can finish the dishes, Bridget. I appreciate you doing it and I'm sorry for shouting at you.

Bridget OK.

Linda opens her magazine.

Linda I'm going to sit here and peruse expensive clothes and take my mind off the day I've had which on the scale of bad days
   is pretty much up there with the day my mother died. Not a good day, children. Be very grateful I am your parent.

Alice I need to talk to you about something. It's important. More important than your bad day, OK? So listen.

Linda What is it?

Alice That girl Amy. In your office. I know her.

Linda Hm?

Alice She was at my school. We were in the same year.

   Beat.

Linda What?

Bridget Which school?

Alice St Saviour's.

   Beat.

Yeah.

Linda Was she
   involved?

Alice She wasn't just involved. She was one of the main ones.

   Linda puts her face in her hands.

What are you doing?

Linda I / can't deal with this.

Bridget What did she say when she saw you?

Alice She didn't recognise me.

Bridget Did you speak to her?

Alice Yeah, I told her who I was. She was like, 'Oh hi, it's so nice to see you.' I wanted to punch her face in.

Linda Look, can we discuss this tomorrow?

Alice looks at her.

I just
    wonder
    if we can maybe talk about it in the morning?

Beat.

Alice I just told you one of the people responsible for ruining my whole life
    works in your office
    and that's all you've got to say?

Linda She didn't ruin your life.

Alice Yes she did.

Linda Alice

Alice Her and the others, yes she fucking did!

Linda Look, it's not that I don't want to talk about it, I just feel like I'm up to here
    with how much emotion I can cope with.

Alice You know what's funny? I thought it might affect you. That's how much of a fucking idiot I am.

Linda Don't / swear!

Alice I thought you'd want to go storming in there and have a go at her!

Linda You want me to have a go at her for sending you a couple of nasty emails when you were at school?

75

Alice Yes! / I want you to want to!

Linda Oh for goodness sake. Just
   grow up would you, Alice? I'm / too tired.

Alice What did you say?

Linda You heard me. You're an adult now. I don't have
to fight your battles for you. You're meant to do that for
yourself. Same as you're meant to earn your own money
and cook your own dinner and / make you own bed and
do your own laundry

Alice I don't ask you to cook me dinner / I never ask you
to cook me dinner!

Linda You live here rent-free. You won't get a job. You
won't even get up before midday. You insist on wearing
that disgusting thing!

Alice Oh, here comes the truth!

Linda Yes, you're right, here comes the truth. Do you
know how much it cost me to send you to university?
And what for? You did some pointless course. Got a
crappy job for a couple of years and now you're back
here doing nothing! How long is it going to go on, Alice?
How much longer is this
   whatever this this
   protest
   how much longer is it going to go on? You don't have
friends. You don't have boyfriends! You're obsessed with
your schooldays! I / did everything you wanted

Alice I've got good reason!

Linda No, you had good reason. Ten years ago! I moved
you out of all those schools. Every time you wanted to go
I let you go. I knew it was wrong but no / you wouldn't
have it.

Alice It's the same thing all over again, isn't it? You're trying to make me feel guilty for something which wasn't my fault!

Linda How am I making you feel guilty?

Alice 'Oh Alice. Why?'

Linda What?

Alice That's what you said. I got home from school and that's what you said to me. 'Oh Alice'. In this voice of disappointment.

Linda That's not what I said.

Alice It's exactly what you said, I remember it because it's burned into my soul like a white hot
    fucking
    flame
    and I can see the look in your eyes as you said it.

    Beat.

'Oh Alice. Why? What a stupid thing to do.'

    Beat.

Stupid Alice. What a stupid fucking slut. Right?

Linda That's not what I think.

Alice Well, I'm sorry if I embarrass you. Sorry I don't live up to your expectations.

Linda You don't embarrass me. / For God's sake, Alice

Alice All you cared about was how it reflected on you! You never thought about what it felt like for me to be humiliated in front of the whole world! Did you?

Linda It wasn't the whole world!

Alice It was my whole world! How dare you say that?

How dare you act as though nothing happened and it didn't matter? My whole life fell apart! And you never even tried to understand!

Linda OK, I get it! I'm a terrible mother! I did everything wrong!

Alice Why do you always do that? You're not the victim! I don't feel sorry for you!

Linda I don't feel sorry for you either!

Alice I fucking know!

Linda Is that what you want? You want me to feel sorry for you? You want me to support this idea that your life
      all that promise
      has just been ruined by something which happened so long ago most people don't ever remember it? You want me to tell you to just give up?

Alice That's not what I want.

Linda Then what do you want?

Alice I want you to be angry with the people who hurt me.

   Beat.

I want you to be so angry with them
      you go out in the middle of the night
      and hunt them down
      and tell them if they ever hurt me again
      you'll slaughter them. I need you
      to blame them.

   Beat.

But instead you blame me.

Linda You just – you had so much going for you. You did so well in your exams. You were talking about Cambridge!

Alice You blamed me when it happened
  then you blamed me all over again for running away.
Because I couldn't be like you. Buy a new lipstick and do
my hair and go back in looking fabulous. Brazen it out.

Linda I just wanted you to accept responsibility. I didn't
want it to happen again.

Alice You think it would happen again? You think I'll
ever
  ever even
  show a man my naked body ever again? Do you think
that's the lesson you needed to teach me? You don't think
the people at school taught me that? Or the hundreds of
messages telling me I was a whore? You don't think that
was the lesson I learned before anything else? You think
I also needed *you* to teach me?

Linda I just wanted to make sure.

  Beat.

Alice I'm going to go upstairs now.

Linda / Alice –

Alice And I'm going to read my book. Just
  leave me alone.

  Alice exits.

Linda Alice?
  Alice!

  *Linda thinks about following her. Then makes a noise
  of despair, defeat.*

  She goes to the fridge, takes out a bottle of wine.

You know there comes a time in your life where you have
to stop expecting your mother to do everything for you,
Bridget. I had to learn how to be a mother all by myself.

Didn't I? And I always believed the best way was to lead by example. I said to myself look, Linda
   you can stay home and do finger-painting and teach your daughter how to sacrifice

Bridget Daughters.

Linda or you can go out there and be inspirational and teach her the importance of fulfilling your own potential.

Bridget Teach them.

Linda But maybe I got it wrong. Maybe I should have been a housewife. Or what do they call it now? A stay-at-home mum.

Bridget Have you been fired?

Linda Don't be silly. I came home early that's all. I wasn't feeling well.

Bridget Is it cancer?

Linda What? No! Haven't you got lines to learn?

Bridget I need to choose a monologue.

Linda Well, go and get on with it. It's getting late.

Linda picks up the magazine again.

Bridget watches her for a moment.

Bridget What about food?

Linda Oh. Right. I'll put something in the oven.

Bridget I'm thinking of doing King Lear. What do you think? Because he goes mad just like Ophelia but he does it in a lot more words. Or there's also Richard the Third who's just mad to begin with. Ah. This is the problem with being a man, you see? You've just got so many options!

Linda is staring into space, as though listening to something.

Mum?
    Are you OK?

Linda Shh. I'm listening.

Bridget To what?

Linda They want me to surrender.

Bridget Who?

Linda They want me to just give up. Give in.

Bridget Who's they?

Linda Who am I?

Bridget You're – my mum. You're Mrs Positive, remember?

Linda You think you're the sun
    and I'm just an orbiting planet. Picking up dirty
knickers. Asking you about your day.

Bridget That's your job, isn't it? That's what mums do.

Linda I'm meant to fade out. Quietly. Without making a
fuss. Cut off all my hair and make other people the centre
of my universe. Well, I'm not going to do that. Do you
hear me? I made it this far. I'm not going to give up. I've
got to go back in there
    and show them that I'm strong.

THIRTEEN

The bathroom.

Alice is looking in the mirror.
    *She rolls up a sleeve of her onesie, to reveal an arm
covered in scars.*

She takes a razor, slices into the flesh.

Blood pours down her arm.

Alice breathes a sigh of relief.

FOURTEEN

Swan offices.
  Boardroom.
  Linda is giving a presentation.
  She has a slideshow set up.

Linda So I've been handed the task of presenting the highlights of the basic premise of this uh – 'Hi-Beautiful' idea – today. How do we launch a campaign which promotes this – uh –

  She clicks a slide.

  anti-ageing cream to the widest possible customer base including young women? How best to present to them the horrors of ageing? To encourage them to feel insecure and therefore buy our product? So. Here's the answer. As I see it.

  She clicks to the next slide.

  It is blank.

We don't.

  Beat.

It's unethical. Immoral. And completely against brand. And before you say anything I can see Dave waving at me to sit down but I'm not going to sit down, Dave, because today I'm making a stand. I don't agree with Hi-Beautiful and I want to talk about something to try and illustrate why, OK?

  She clicks on to a slide picture of her in a glittery dress accepting an award.

When the women in our research groups talked about feeling invisible, I told myself oh that will never happen to me. I've won awards. I'll always be important. But even then I could hear them. These – insidious – voices – in my head telling me, Linda, it's already happening. It happens at home when I ask my daughter to tidy her bedroom. It happens when I go to the mechanic and ask a question about my car and he rolls his eyes at me

belittles me for not knowing something which once upon a time he would have enjoyed 'explaining' with a little flirt and a wink. It happens when I walk down the street with my husband and I see his head turn

his gaze drift

he tunes out the sound of my voice because there's an attractive young woman walking down the street towards us and for some reason

my husband can't walk past an attractive young woman without staring at her. I try to pretend it doesn't bother me. I try to pretend he loves me so it doesn't matter because it's only looking, isn't it? Why does it matter if men would rather look at a younger woman? Why should I care? I asked myself this question over and over. And I kept on thinking about my husband. In fact let's talk about my husband for a bit shall we? My husband's name is Neil! He's a pretty average man. To be honest. Always has been. And when we were younger – if you'd seen us together you'd have thought oh, hasn't he done well! And I enjoyed that feeling. I didn't mind that he was average because he was also loyal and steady and dependable. Once upon a time. But here's the thing: as my husband got older? He got more attractive. Back then he was punching above his weight. Now? He thinks he's a rock star! And why? Because men get more fuckable as they get older don't they? And the world says well, yes that's normal because men still have sperm don't they and add to their ever-potent sperm the fact that as they get older they get more powerful more wealthy

whereas you Linda

you might be more powerful and more wealthy than you were twenty years ago but you? You're just a dried up old husk! Why would anyone want to fuck you once your womb stops working? SIT DOWN DAVE, I'm talking. Amy asked me to do a PowerPoint I'm doing a fucking PowerPoint and I'm asking you this: what does getting older mean when you're a woman? It's not a mid-life crisis and a sports car. Is it? It's not swapping your wife for a younger model. Or taking up golf. Or starting a band. Is it? It's not CEO. Or joining the board. It's not silver fox and second time round no no no. Old for a woman means worthless. Pointless. Vanishing. Of course we're terrified. You tell us we peak at sixteen and its downhill all the way from there and and and now

having spent the best part of two decades dedicated to the cause of getting women to feel beautiful no matter who they are

despite the fact I've won awards

you're not listening to me. You've all stopped listening. Your heads have been turned by a girl in the street and I'm not going to let that happen. Do you hear me? I'm grabbing your heads

with both hands

and I'm fucking turning you back towards me and I'm making you look. Look! Look at me! Listen to me! I'm not just going to sit down and be ignored. I haven't worked this hard to be pushed aside at the last hurdle. I'm standing here. I'm making you listen. I will not disappear!

Her voice through the mike, too close, sends the high pitch noise reverberating through the sound system. Linda stumbles back from the podium.

End of Act One.

Act Two

ONE

Music plays. It's Buddy Clark and Ray Noble's song 'Linda'.
   Kitchen.
   Linda, in a silky dressing gown, is preparing a delicious breakfast for three. She mouths along to the female part in the song. Acts it out a bit. Having fun.
   After a while, Alice enters, wearing a coat over the onesie. Stands watching Linda dance. Scowls.

Linda You're up! Good morning!

   Alice doesn't reply.

Are you still not speaking to me?

Alice I'm speaking to you. I've just got nothing to say.

Linda Are you going into the office?

Alice Yes.

Linda Good for you!

   Beat.

Here, take a seat. I'm not going in today. I made breakfast!

Alice I'm not hungry. Why aren't you going in?

Linda I'm practising the art of 'show 'em what they're missing'. See how long it takes Dave to call and tell me things are falling apart. Beg me to come back.

Alice OK.

Linda I give him till Friday lunchtime.

Alice Even after your little speech?

Linda Oh. Well.

Alice Apparently you went mental in front of the board.

Linda I didn't go mental! I simply told them all a few home truths and restated the objectives of the brand. In the early days of True Beauty, Dave and me used to fight like cat and dog. Trust me in the long run he's going to thank me.

Alice heads out.

Alice OK well. Good luck with that. See you later.

Linda Will you be home for tea?

Alice Nope. I'll be late.

Linda Have you got plans?

Alice Mind your own business.

Bridget enters in her school uniform, just as Alice heads out.

Linda Do you want to take something to eat on the way?

Bridget Where's Dad?

Linda I'm proud of you!

But Alice is gone.

Bridget I need to talk to him. I chose my speech.

Linda Sit down and have some breakfast. Your father's left for school.

Bridget What's all this?

Linda I made breakfast.

Bridget Why?

Linda What do you mean why? Why not?

Bridget heads out.

Bridget Weird.

Linda Don't you want something?

Bridget Nah, gotta go. And don't forget I'm going to Fiona's after drama club to practise. Her mum said she'd give me a lift home if it's late.

Linda I can come and pick you up?

Bridget No thanks. No need.

Bridget takes a pancake and is gone.

Linda Have a good day!

Linda sits alone in the kitchen.

She shakes her head a little.

The unwanted breakfast spread out before her. The jaunty music plays.

The kitchen seems empty.

She looks at her phone. She waits. Nothing happens.

Suddenly, she stands and hurries upstairs.

TWO

Dave's office.
  Linda and Dave.

Linda I said to myself it's petty. Staying away to show them what disasters befall them in your absence. You know?

Dave Linda –

Linda Whatever our differences

I care deeply about this company Neil and I'm not just going to abandon you at this critical time because of a minor disagreement about direction.

Dave Dave.

Linda What?

Dave You called me Neil.

Linda No I didn't. And yes I'm concerned my voice isn't being heard but it's certainly not going to be heard if I'm sitting in my kitchen doing nothing is it? So. I'm back. I've been thinking about how to adapt the outreach programme to fit in with Hi-Beautiful. And you'll be pleased to know that I feel confident I can come up with a solution.

Dave I'm afraid it's not quite that simple, Linda.

Linda Really?

Dave What?

Linda Why not?

Dave We have to deal with what happened. Don't we?

Now. I've spoken to Carol and we've come up with a couple of options about how to proceed. I'm going to start with my preferred choice and we'll go from there. OK?

Linda I mean

Dave Option one. You pop to the doctor and get yourself signed off for a bit.

Linda The doctor?

Dave Hear me out, OK? You're obviously feeling overwhelmed and Carol thinks some of this reaction might be due to over-exertion. She says HR are keen to be supportive so if you're prepared to go and get some help to uh – feel better – well then we can manage perfectly well without you for a bit.

Linda But there's nothing wrong with me! Yes, I've been under some pressure. There's been a a situation at home but
I've dealt with it. I'm dealing with it. And it's really much better for me if I can keep busy. There's a lot of work to be done.

Dave OK then, fine. In that case we'll move to option two.

Linda Great.

Dave We're going to ask you to step down as Ambassador before the Munich trip.

Linda stares at him.

The Board don't feel it's appropriate for you to be presenting the product to the Germans after what happened. You're too high risk.

Linda Yes I went a bit over the top in my speech, Dave, but that's just me isn't it? I'm passionate. I've always been high risk.

Dave Yes / but

Linda It's my being 'high risk' which has taken this company to the global market.

Dave Everyone admires the work you've done for us. But let's not go over old ground shall we?

Linda I took your crappy little soaps and creams and turned them into an international movement.

Dave Linda!

Linda Without me you'd be sitting on the bottom shelf in the chemist's gathering dust. Dave. I'm the face of this company whether you like it or not. And there was nothing wrong with my making a stand!

Dave You stood up in front of the Board and started speculating about who may or may not want to fuck you, Linda!

Linda Oh so what? I was using a personal example.

Dave Well, I found your personal example extremely inappropriate!

Linda Fine! I'm sorry you were offended! I'll apologise to the Board for any specific comments which upset them but what I will not apologise for is is my

passionate defence of the objectives and aspirations of this brand. Which you have put under threat. Because you're like a you're like a magpie who found something shiny and forgot about his nest. Aren't you?

I don't care what you say, I know what's really going on here, David Hodges.

Beat.

You forget how long I've known you.

Dave Be very careful, Linda.

Linda No, I don't think I will be careful. I think I'll go back to my office and start working out how to make an outreach programme for this campaign you've chosen. I'm going to take what you've done, and turn it into something positive. Something beautiful. Something to help people. I'm going to show you I can still make a difference. I'm still relevant. You watch. I'm relevant!

THREE

Linda's office.

Linda paces up and down, planning a speech.

Linda We are redefining what the world thinks of as beautiful. We've had enough of being told who we look. How we look. Wait.

A high-pitched whining noise comes from somewhere.

She stands for a moment, as though lost.

Then:

A knock on the door.

Beat.

Linda Come in?

The door opens. It's Luke.

Oh. Luke. Come in.

Luke Hi!

Linda Sorry, I was in a world of my own.

He comes in.

Luke Sorry to bother you. Got my timesheet for you to sign.

Linda Sure.

Luke How you doing?

Linda Not too bad. How are you?

Luke I'm good thanks, Linda. Here.

She looks down at the timesheet.

You look nice.

Linda Oh. Thank you!

Luke I love that colour on you. Makes you look I dunno. Softer.

Linda Really?

She absent-mindedly signs the sheet.

Luke Mm. Oh great thanks.

Linda Here you go.

Luke That's brilliant. Thanks, Linda. Do you need anything?

Linda I'm sorry?

Luke I was just asking you if you need anything.

Linda Gosh.

Luke Are you OK?

Linda It's just
such a long time since anyone asked me what I need.
You sort of
caught me off guard.

Luke I just meant
you know, a tea? Or a coffee?

Beat.

Linda Oh.

Luke You sure you're OK?

Linda I feel a bit faint.

Luke Shit, Linda. Here. Let me help you. Sit down.

Linda Could you just
no I don't want to sit down I just
could you just hold me up?

Luke Sure.

He grabs her arms. Holds her up.

Linda Oh that's nice.

Luke Like this?

Linda Yes, that's perfect.

Beat.

Luke You sure you don't want me to get someone?

Linda No that's good. That's exactly what I need.

Luke I think you should maybe go home.

Linda You're helping.

Luke OK.

Linda Just stay like that. Please?

Luke No worries.

Linda The work isn't done, Luke. You see? That's the problem. But I'm just
I feel very tired.

Luke Try to breathe.

Linda I don't think they have any possible way to understand how much
it takes
to keep going.

Luke Uh-huh.

Linda Someone wants that idea on his desk by eight. And someone else needs their uniform washed by eight thirty. So you push through, don't you? Because you imagine
the day will come where everyone will appreciate you.

Luke We cannot know what the future brings.

Linda Is anyone ever going to say THANK YOU?

Luke Shush. Hey. You know what this is don't you, Lin? This is the best moment of your life. This is an opportunity.

Linda Is it?

Luke You need to let go of your data.

Linda Huh?

Luke I know it feels painful. Of course it does. Our attachment to the material world
    to our ambitions
    emotions
    perceptions
    experiences
    all that data we've believed is so important for so long
    letting go of it can be incredibly painful. Blistering.
But here you are. Staring into the Abyss. This is it. This is your moment. Here is where your life begins. Right here. Right now. Look at it. Stare it in the face. Know
    that you are just an insignificant speck of dust.
Nothing you can do or say can change anything. You're irrelevant. Let awareness of that thought wash over you
    freeing you from the speculation of possibility and the painfulness of human attachment. We are nobodies. And none of this matters.

Linda I'm changing the world
    one girl at a time

Luke The world doesn't need to change, Lin. It's fine just as it is.

Linda No.

Luke Just as it's meant to be.

Linda How can it be fine?

Luke I know, right? It sounds crazy. But it's true. I used to be a very angry person. I wanted to fight and like change stuff. And then one day someone I know learned a great wisdom and I finally understood: fighting's not the answer.

Linda I'm making a better world for my daughters to grow up in.

Luke Are you?

Linda I created and developed a brand which made women feel beautiful no matter what! I've dedicated my life to it, Luke. I've spent more time in this office than anywhere else.

Luke And? Where has it got you?

Linda Don't start telling me I've never had an impact! You're not involved in the world of beauty so you might not know but you go out there to other companies and you say the name Linda Wilde and you'll know exactly what I mean! You don't win awards for nothing, OK?

Luke OK / OK.

Linda I can still make things happen, Luke. I don't care what they say.

Luke I believe you.

Linda I can change things.

Luke Go on then.

Linda steps in towards him.

Kisses him.

Linda See?
Sorry.
I don't know why I did that.

Luke It's OK.

Linda I don't know what I was thinking.

Luke I don't mind. Here –

They look at each other.

He pulls her back towards her. They snog for a bit. Then:

You wanna go up to the storeroom?

Linda Why?

Luke It's quiet in there. No one around. You can lock the door.

Beat.

Linda Can you?

From somewhere, faintly, the sound of beating wings. They do not hear it.

He reaches out his hand. She takes it.

FOUR

Linda's office.

Amy puts a bottle of product down on Linda's desk. Waits a moment.
Then takes a moment to imagine this office is hers. Looks out of the window.

Then goes back over to the desk and writes a note to go with the bottle.

Alice enters. She has the head pulled up on her onesie, no clothes covering it now.

Amy Hey, have you seen Linda? I can't find her anywhere. I want to give her this!

Alice When my mother was seven. My grandmother committed suicide.

Amy Sorry?

Alice Their house was near a river and apparently she just left in the middle of the night, went out on to the bridge, climbed over the railings and jumped. Didn't even think about it.

Amy Is this like a charity thing? Cos I haven't got my purse.

Alice It's not.
    The repercussions of our actions
    impulse decisions made in the moment
    keep vibrating through the cosmos

Amy Uh-oh.

Alice   on and on until we make a choice.

Amy This is a wind-up right?

Alice I'm making that choice today.

Amy Did Luke put you up to this?

Alice I'm making a choice to speak my truth.

Amy What about the outfit? I don't get it.

Alice Let the anger rage. The desire rage. The pride rage.

Amy Wow you really learned it.

Alice While we relax like sky.

Amy I should get back to my desk.

Alice Once upon a time there were two girls who went to the same school. And their names were Amy and Alice.

    Beat.

    They weren't best friends or anything. But they always got on OK. Didn't they?

Beat.

Amy I think so.

Alice Until one day Alice broke up with her boyfriend Damon and he was very upset. So he decided to share something private with the whole school. I don't need to tell you the next part. Do I?

Beat.

There was a particularly vicious message about how I should be so ashamed I should go home and kill myself, remember that? That was one of yours.

Amy It wasn't just me.

Alice I thought about that one a lot. You know? That was the one that really stuck in me because of my grandma who I never met. Cos I'd never understood why she did it before that desire to just
    make everything stop. How else can I stop the endless messages? The kids screaming SLAG at me everywhere I go? How can I stop all those fucking eyes
    looking at those fucking pictures?

Amy I didn't know about your grandma, Alice.

Alice Why did you do it? I just want to understand. And then I can let it go.

Beat.

    Help me let it go.

Amy I don't know what you want me to say. We were just kids! It was years ago! I didn't hate you or anything. I thought you were cool. And if I said those awful things to you which I don't remember saying but if I did then I think all I meant was just trying to express
    how I'd feel. You know. If I was you.

Beat.

We didn't want you to leave Alice. We all felt bad when you just vanished like that. / Maybe if we'd known

Alice I didn't vanish. I moved schools. And three weeks in, Damon found out where I was and sent the photos to a guy in my new class. You'd be amazed how predictable people can be in their reactions to things. By the third school I was almost ready for it

Amy That's terrible.

Alice I tried to get away. Go to university. But it never stopped. Men's eyes. Following me wherever I went. And not just looks. The little comments. 'Alright sexy'. 'Morning sweetheart'. It was like being surrounded by a pack of animals!

And eventually it got to the point where every time a van beeped its horn at me

or a builder whistled or

or the checkout guy told me I've got nice eyes

I wanted to fucking scream at every single man who said any tiny thing only I couldn't because I'm weak. I couldn't because I knew from experience that if you piss men off

Amy covers her face with her hands.

if you piss them off and you're a girl
you're going to get hurt.

Beat.

And then one day I found this in a second-hand shop

She means the onesie.

and I found out
when I wear this
they don't see me any more. People don't see a young woman and when men don't see a young woman they

don't feel the need to pass comment. They might look but I know they're looking at the skunk. Not me. When I wear this

I become invisible.

Beat.

Amy I don't know what to say.

Alice You could say sorry?

Beat.

Amy I'm sorry if what I did upset you, Alice. I honestly never thought you'd take it so personally. OK?

Beat.

And like. Just so you know? Men beeping at you and all that? Giving you compliments in the street. That's got nothing to do with those silly photos. I promise you. That's normal yeah? Every girl gets that. You should try being a blonde!

FIVE

Home. Evening.

Linda has a drink in her hand and is looking for a lighter.

Linda (*on the phone*) No I need at least thirty. We want to make a scene around the shores of a lake and I want a whole crowd. No, they've all got to be women over the age of fifty. Oh, and I need to find out how much it's going to cost to get a live swan.

Bridget enters. Waits.

Beat.

Then I'll call the Queen and ask her!

Yes, I want it delivered. This has literally got to be the most amazing visual I've ever created. I'm going to have to knock their socks off. So.

OK, great. I'll talk to you tomorrow.

She hangs up. Turns to Bridget.

Woo! Someone's on fire!

Bridget What?

Linda Me! I'm on creative fire! Ideas ideas ideas just pinging around my brain!

Linda does a weird kind of dance.

Where's Alice? Did she come back yet?

Bridget No.

Linda Fuck your homework. Let's bake a massive cake together and then eat the whole thing in one go. Amyamyam.

Linda mimes eating a whole cake in one go. Bridget looks at her.

Bridget You're being weird again. But in a new way. What's happened to you?

Linda What's happened is that I've had a profound understanding of the unexpected nature of being alive, Bridget. You cannot know what the future holds. Did you know that?

Bridget Where's Dad?

Linda Ugh. I don't know.

Bridget What do you mean, you don't know?

Linda Why don't you ask him? Why is it always me who has to answer to everything?!

Bridget His phone's off. I've left him ten voicemails. Where is he?

Linda Send him an email.

Bridget TELL ME!

Linda For God's sake there's nothing to tell. Your father's
   gone on a school trip. Someone was off sick. He had to fill in at the last minute.

Bridget When will he be back?

Linda I don't know. A few days.

Bridget If Dad's dead I want to know.

Linda What are you on about?

Bridget WHAT DID HE DIE OF?

Linda He's not dead!

Bridget Has he become gay?

Linda What?

Bridget Has dad become gay and left you?

Linda No. Quite the opposite in fact.

The doorbell goes.

Bridget What does that mean?

Linda Nothing. Alice probably forgot her key again. Let her in, would you?

Bridget If I get the door will you tell me?

Linda I'll tell you later. Let your sister in.

Bridget exits.

Linda takes out her phone. Dials. While she waits she goes to the cupboard. Takes out the whisky. Pours herself a generous helping.

Oh hello, yes could you get me the number for Buckingham Palace?

Uh, if there's a number for general enquiries that'll do.

Bridget comes back in, followed by Stevie. Linda is still busy with the whisky.

Yes I'll hold.

Bridget Mum?

Linda I'm just on the phone.

Bridget Dad's friend is here. I said he was away but

Linda turns.

Linda Oh.

Beat.

Stevie Hi.

Linda Hi.

Beat.

She hangs up her phone.

Bridget? I need to talk to Daddy's friend.

Bridget Why?

Linda Take your tea and go upstairs.

Bridget Is this to do / with where he is?

Linda Do as you're told. Bridget. Now!

Bridget does as she's told. She leaves, staring at Stevie as she goes.

When she is gone and out of earshot:

If you're looking for Neil he's not here.

Stevie I know.

I'm not looking for him. I'm looking for you.

Linda For me?

Stevie I want to talk to you.

Linda Oh. I see.

Stevie About Neil.

Linda Well yes.

Beat.

Do you want to sit down?

Stevie I won't take up much of your time I just felt after the other day maybe there were some things I needed to explain.

Linda I might just get myself a drink if you don't mind.

Stevie Sure.

Linda Do you want one?

Stevie I'm OK thanks.

Linda I don't mind.

Stevie I mean. OK then. Yes please.

Linda Whisky OK? It's not expensive. I got it on my way back from Munich. I travel a lot for work. Did Neil ever mention that?

Stevie shakes her head.

No?

I wanted to come to your gig but he told me not to. Sorry it's not a gig is it? 'Open-mic night'.

Beat.

When is it again?

Stevie We're not doing it. The band. It's finished.

Linda Aw.

Stevie So.

Linda You could go solo? That's what people do, isn't it? Quit the band. Go it alone.

Stevie I'm no good on my own.

Linda That's not true. You've got a lovely voice.

Stevie What?

Linda I've seen your little music videos. I stayed up all night looking at pictures you've posted of your own face on the internet. And then I had to go and give a presentation at work. And you know what? It didn't go very well.

Stevie I'm – sorry to hear that.

Linda brings the drinks over.

Linda Here.

Stevie Thank you.

Linda lights a fag.

Stevie downs the whole drink in one. Coughs for a bit. Linda watches her, curious.

Linda So you're not pregnant then?

Stevie What?

Stevie coughs a bit more.

No!

Linda OK then. Good.

Stevie Me and Neil are a hundred per cent finished.

Linda Did he tell you to say this?

Stevie No! I swear to you.

Linda Then what is there to explain?

Stevie OK. The thing is
    I just wanted to tell you because
    my father was
    is

Linda Your father?

Stevie Please let me say it.

Beat.

Linda OK.

Stevie When my father was married to my mother
    there was my mother
    sitting in the kitchen weeping or when he came home late
    screaming at him demanding answers and him unreachable
    a kind word from my father was like gold dust. You know?
    I swore I would never do to another woman what his women did to my mother. I remember thinking: why don't they care? How can they not mind about his wife? His child?

Linda Ha!

Stevie One day my mother had enough. And in our village the story was 'poor man, his wife kicked him out'. He sent money once in a while but always begrudging. As though I was a leftover
    a remnant of a life he wished he never had. And I suppose as a result of this my relationship to men has always been
    difficult.

Beat.

If I went into all the details, Linda, you'd never believe me. Too many bad things have happened.

Linda I might.

Stevie No, it's too much. They wear you down. You start to believe you're a very low person. And my mother too

I wish I could say it brought us close but the truth is I feel a desperation not to end up like her. A fear that one day I'll be sitting in a kitchen screaming and demanding answers because all men are liars and love itself is a lie but at the same time I want a man to love me. I want it so badly. And when I met Neil

it's hard to explain but I need to try, Linda, because I'm not like those other women. It's not that I didn't care about you. I did. I do. I just

somehow when it was happening to me

I believed I was different.

Linda I thought you were going to explain how it happened.

Stevie I'm just trying / to

Linda I want to know how it happened.

Beat.

Stevie I'm sorry.

Linda Tell me how it started. You were rehearsing in the band. And what? He made a pass at you?

Stevie No!

Linda No?

Stevie That's not how it was. I promise. Please –

Linda How was it then?

Beat.

Tell me. Exactly what happened.

Stevie stares away.

Or leave.

Stevie looks at Linda.

Stevie I was the one who did the chasing. I flirted. I pushed. I asked him out for drinks after rehearsal. I told him he was incredible. Talented. Strong. I believed all those things of course in a way. But I also understood what he needed to hear. And one night we got drunk and I kissed him. He felt very guilty. He didn't speak to me for days.

Linda How noble.

Stevie But then I guess
he called me and we

. . .

Stevie turns away.

Linda Fucked in my bed?

Stevie This isn't going as I planned.

Linda No?

Stevie I know what you're thinking but it's not the truth! I don't want to steal him. It wasn't about him. It was about
about a vision of the life I'd have with him. A man who is older and wiser and drives a car and and knows about politics. Someone who could, you know. Look after me.

Linda I bought him that car.

Stevie Oh.

Linda Carry on.

Stevie All I mean is I'm twenty-seven years old and I work in a call centre. I earn just enough money to pay my rent and buy cheap food from the supermarket. But when I was with Neil

Linda You're twenty-seven?

Stevie Yes.

Linda You look younger.

Beat.

Stevie Thanks.

Linda Did he say we never had sex any more?

Stevie No.

Linda Did he say he didn't love me?

Stevie He never said anything like that. All he ever said was you were this amazing woman with this unbelievably successful career. And that you were a fantastic mother.

Beat.

If you blame someone for what happened
blame me. Neil spends his whole life being
you know. You're a very impressive person, Linda.
Maybe it's hard sometimes
I think he enjoyed being the impressive one for a bit.
You know? I got to be the young and wild and beautiful
girl like in a movie and Neil
for once in his life
Neil got to be the hero.

Pause.

Linda goes to the window. She looks out. Stevie watches her.

I'm sorry. I hope I didn't make it worse.

Beat.

Linda Who was I?

Beat.

Stevie I don't know what you mean.

Linda You said you were the girl. And he was the hero. I'm asking: who was I?

Stevie You were no one. I don't mean, I just mean there wasn't a
    name. You were just
    in the story of me and him you were
    no one.

SIX

The girls' bedroom. Night.

Bridget is in bed.
    Alice is packing.

Bridget I think you should wait a few days. They're saying there might be a hurricane.

Alice I'll be fine. Do you want my new iPhone?

Bridget You're not taking your iPhone?

Alice Do you want it or not?

Bridget You might need it.

Alice Not where I'm going.

Bridget Are you sure?

Alice I don't need it. Take it.

Bridget Wow. Thanks! Where are you going to stay?

Alice I'm crashing at Luke's. He's finally getting the last bit of money he needs for his ticket to Bali so there's going to be a spare bed in his house. And when I've saved up enough I'm going to go join him.

Bridget In Bali?

Alice That's our spiritual home. There's a big commune by the beach and everyone's completely non-judgemental. Here. You can read the book.

Bridget Is Luke your boyfriend?

Alice Of course not. No! Relationships are just a part of the illusion.

Bridget But if nothing's real
why do you need to go to Bali? I mean
surely Bali's not real. And it's so far away.

Alice It's not just about reality it's about being in the moment and not thinking about the past. I want to be someone new. And if I stay here and live with her I'm never going to get away from it.

Bridget Mum just wants you to be happy.

Alice No she doesn't. She thinks I'm a failure. And I'm sick of trying to live up to her expectations all the time. You can be whoever you want. Remember that, OK? You don't have to be a version of her.

Bridget You are coming back?

Beat.

Alice I don't want to be out there feeling guilty because I'm not sending emails home. The point is to let go of the past. I'm not going to be Alice Collier any more. I'm going to be someone new.

Bridget You can't just forget about us.

Alice I'm not forgetting about you but
you're too young to understand. I need to do this. For me.

Pause.

Bridget?

Bridget What?

Alice Say something.

Bridget Mum loves you.

Alice No she doesn't.

Bridget I love you.

Alice Love
   is just an idea we're attached to. Now shut your eyes.
I need to get changed.

Bridget Are you
   are you taking it off?

Alice I'm taking it off.

Bridget But what about the magic?

Alice I'm letting go of unhelpful beliefs.

Bridget What if something bad happens?

Alice I can't be responsible for everything any more. I
need to look after myself now. Shut your eyes.

   Bridget covers her eyes with her hands.

   As Alice takes off the onesie:

The beach in Bali goes on for miles. White powder sand
and turquoise sea. Sitting under a coconut tree. The sun
in the sky. And a group of human beings with no
attachments to right or wrong. Or love. Or beauty. Who
just exist in the moment. Doesn't that sound wonderful?

   *Under the onesie, Alice is wearing a grubby wife-
   beater and boxer shorts, both stained with old blood.
   Her body is covered with welts, scars old and new, the
   result of years of self-harming.*

Bridget It's easy to be in the moment when you're on the
beach.

Alice You don't get it.

Alice pulls jogging bottoms and a jumper on. As:

I'm going to wait till Mum's in bed, OK? I don't want any more drama.

Bridget You can't not tell her you're going.

Alice Why not? OK, you can open.

Beat.

Bridget You look different.

Alice Good. See? It's working already.

Bridget You can't just go without saying goodbye to Mum. What if you never see her again? What if she dies and you never make it up? / You'll never forgive yourself.

Alice Stop going on at me!
I'm not going to keep chasing the data that I need my mother's approval in order to be happy in life! Maybe my mother will never approve of me! So what?

Suddenly: the iPhone rings.

Bridget Oh!

Alice Who is it?

Bridget holds it up for Alice to see.

Bridget It's my dad.

SEVEN

The bathroom. Night.

Linda stands in front of the mirror. For a long time. She stares at herself.

For a long time she sees herself as she always has.

She takes out some Hi-Beautiful.

Applies it to her face and neck.

Stares at herself.

And then, after a while, something changes.

EIGHT

Pub. Night.

Amy and Luke are having a drink.

There is an envelope on the table.
  Amy is reading from a phone.

Amy 'Hi sexy. Thanks for a good time earlier. Can't stop thinking about you naked. Let me know if you want to go to the store cupboard again. Luke.'

Luke What did I tell you?
  Read the reply.

Amy Where's the reply?

Luke Scroll up.

Amy You're disgusting. You know that?

Luke Hey. I had to make sure you believed me.

Amy 'Dear Luke. I had a lovely time too. Linda.'

Luke See?

Amy I can't believe you actually did it. I mean
  I do
  because you showed me this but otherwise? No
fucking way. No way. What about your spiritual beliefs?

Luke What about them? I told you. I didn't do it for the money. I wouldn't do that to Linda. I respect her too

much. But we had a moment. One thing led to another as they say. And since as it turns out I won our bet I thought
well
my training will further the enlightenment of the human race. I'm sure Linda would support that. What are you doing?

Amy Just forwarding it.

Luke What?

He reaches for the phone – she moves it out the way.

Amy Only to myself. Calm down!

Luke What for?

Amy Because I might need to prove it to Jonny.

Luke Why?

Amy Why do you think?

She picks up the envelope.

We're meant to be saving up for our honeymoon.

Luke I don't think you should tell Jonny, Amy. You know what this shit's like. You tell one person
they tell one person
it could end up hurting Linda.

Amy So what?

Luke So that's not why I did it.

Amy You love her.

Luke Piss off.

Amy You're in love with her.

Luke I'm not in love with her but she's actually
I don't know.

Amy Oh my God. You actually do love her!

Luke I don't love her. I was just going to say it was actually a pretty nice time. We had a very spiritual connection.

Are you going to give it to me?

Amy Let me read them again. Hang on

Luke Amy –

She is reading again.

He shakes his head.

She laughs.

Laughs again.

Amy Fuck.

Luke OK, you've read them now give me my money.

Amy Fine. Take your money, you dirty bastard. Now you can piss off to Bali and leave me on my own with the bitch.

Luke Thank you. Now please promise you won't show those emails to anyone.

Amy Fine.

Luke Promise?

Amy On Linda's life.

Luke Amy.

Amy What? OK OK, I promise.

Luke Delete them. Will you?

Amy First thing in the morning.

Luke It's going to be some serious bad karma for you if you don't.

Amy Are you putting a curse on me?

Luke I'm just saying.

Amy I'm not going to tell anyone. Honestly, Luke, I've got better things to think about. I've got to make a decision about my flowers. Choose napkins. Go for a dress fitting. Jonny's bloody booking this stag night to Prague which I'm not exactly pleased about and I've got ten pounds to shift before June which might not sound like a lot but when you're already slim it's a big ask.

Luke You've got a lot on.

Amy You're not kidding. I mean yes, I'm getting married just about according to schedule because I said twenty-six and no later but that gives me three years, Luke. Three years to get promoted as much as possible before I reach optimum baby age. If you go much past twenty-nine you risk being phased out in the workplace and your body doesn't ping back into shape. And if you don't ping back into shape you could end up being fat for the rest of your life. And if you're a fat woman then you actually earn less, did you know that? They did a survey in America? And it found very thin women earned something like forty thousand dollars more a year than fat women. Which means once you've had a baby it only stands to reason you're going to earn less money. I need to ping back into shape, Luke. It's very important for my future.

Luke I think you need to chill out.

Amy Are you kidding me? Don't you know anything? I don't want to be a sad old spinster with no kids who only cares about her job! Luke. Right? And I don't want to be a fucking housewife with three great kids but absolutely no life outside of all that. I don't want people to feel sorry for me. And everyone knows you're only truly happy and successful if you have all of the above! And everyone knows that having all of the above is almost impossible. OK? I want all of the above! All of the above! Oh God –

Amy bursts into tears. Then she breathes hard and pulls herself together.

The following is almost a mantra to bring her emotion back under control:

I want a successful career. I want a nice husband. I want a big house. I want two kids. I want to have my own office
     high up in a fancy building with a view looking out over the river!
     / I want

Luke You want to be Linda.

Amy What?

Luke You basically want to be Linda.

Amy Don't be insanio. Urgh. Are you joking? I never ever want to be that crazy bitch. I'd rather die.

NINE

Home. Early morning.

Bridget in her pyjamas, is staring out of the window.
     Linda enters, wearing a green dress suit from the year 2000.

Linda I found it! Look! It was up in the attic and see?

She pats her behind.

It still fits perfectly. Told you. God, the work I had to do to get back into this after you were born, Bridget. You were such an enormous baby!

Beat.

Well? What do you think?

Bridget doesn't respond.

Bridget Alice has gone.

Linda She's keen.

Bridget Not to work. Gone. Packed all her stuff. Moved out.

Linda What?

Bridget So you got what you wanted.

Linda How do you mean?

Beat.

Bridget She left her onesie. It's lying on her bed like a
        like a skin. Like Alice
    with all the blood and air sucked out of her so there's
nothing left but fur and ears.

Linda That's a good sign, isn't it? Maybe she's feeling
better.

Bridget She said it was keeping us safe.

Linda That's superstitious nonsense and you know it.

Bridget Is it?

Linda Where's she gone?

Bridget Some boy she met in your office has got a spare
room. And she said she never wants to see you again so
what was the point of saying goodbye?

Linda What boy from my office?

Bridget They believe in this religion together. It's all
about nothing being real and everything's an illusion.

Linda Luke?

Bridget That's it.

Linda She's gone with Luke?

Bridget She's crashing at his for a bit. Then they're going to Bali.

> *Beat.*

She never wants to see you again.

Linda Are they together?

Bridget No. They're just friends. She stopped believing in love. I thought you'd be upset but you're not, are you?

Linda I don't know what to feel.

Bridget Yeah, because there's something wrong with you.

Linda What do you mean?

Bridget That's why she wants to get away from you.

Linda Is she coming back into the office?

Bridget I doubt it.

Linda But she's coming back home?

Bridget Are you stupid? How many times do I have to say it? She's not coming home. She never wants to see you again. Ever!

Linda Oh, she's just saying that! You know what she's like!

Bridget I think she's right. To escape you.

Linda What's the matter with you? Why are you talking to me like that?

Bridget Because I spoke to Dad.

Beat.

Linda When?

Bridget He's not on a school trip.

Beat.

He's staying with his friend Martin.

Linda And?

Bridget And he wants to come back home.

Beat.

Are you going to let him?

Linda What else did he say?

Bridget He said you two were having some problems and *you* needed some space. He's trying to make out like it's his fault but it's not, is it? What did you do to him?

Linda Nothing.

Bridget Why is everyone leaving?

Linda Your father's right. We just need some space / for a bit.

Bridget He didn't say we. He said *you*. I know he wants to be here. When are you going to let him come back?

Linda I don't know.

Bridget You're driving everyone away!

Linda Bridget –

Bridget Why are you doing this?

Linda I can't explain it. Your father
        did something
        and I'm finding it very difficult to forgive him.

Beat.

Bridget What did he do?

Linda It doesn't matter what he did.

Bridget Yes it does!

Linda Nothing he does has any reflection on how he feels about you. And it shouldn't affect your future relationship with men. OK? I don't want it to make you feel like
you need to do things to compensate.

Bridget What are you talking about? What did he do?

Beat.

Tell me!

Linda He just
I just felt
he was spending too much time
concentrating on the band. That's all.

Bridget That's it? You kicked him out of the house for that?

Linda I don't know.

Bridget You're at work all hours of the day. You go away for weeks on end. And you're cross with Dad because of his band?

Linda I don't know how to explain it.

Bridget Then don't. Just call him and tell him to come back. You find some space. You go somewhere else!

Linda Oh, that would be nice wouldn't it?

Bridget Why not? You don't give a shit about me. If you did you wouldn't have got rid of my dad for no reason!

Linda It's not that simple.

Bridget Alice is right about you. You do things for yourself and just say they're to help other people. Well, you know what? You don't help anyone. You never have.

Linda I don't help anyone!

Bridget You think all you need to do is tell us we're beautiful and we'll be happy, well you're wrong and you're deluded because we don't want to be told we're beautiful. We never did. We want to be told we're we're
    funny. Or clever. Or worth something. We want to be recognised for who we actually are not just who you want us to be.

Linda Well, I can certainly hear your sister's influence in that little attack!

Bridget Yes, because it all makes sense to me now. I finally understand why I hate myself so much. It's because of you.

Linda Bridget! You don't hate yourself!

Bridget Yes I do! I hate everything about myself!

Beat.

Linda OK, well I honestly don't see the point of continuing this conversation. I can understand you being upset but I'm not your punchbag, Bridget. I need to get to work. I've got a lot to organise.

Bridget Well, I'm going to call Dad and tell him to come home.

Linda No you're not.

Bridget Yes I am, so if you want some space from him then I suggest you go somewhere else. Because you're not welcome here.

Linda OK / Bridget.

Bridget And then I need to get ready for my audition.

Beat.

Linda Oh!

Bridget Which is today. By the way.

Linda I'm so sorry. I knew it was today I just completely I've had so much going / on I

Bridget It's fine don't worry about it. I didn't expect you to remember. I didn't expect you to wish me luck. Or give me a lift. Or help me do lines. You know what I expected from you, Mum?
I expected nothing.

TEN

Dave's office.

Dave stands by the window.
Linda is standing by her desk, holding some papers.
Outside the wind is blowing a gale.

Dave Well?
What do you have to say for yourself?

Linda I don't understand. You fired him?

Dave I didn't need to fire him, Linda. He's gone. Didn't even say goodbye. Dawn went to tidy up the mess he left on his desk and found those. I tell you one thing I'm going to make damn sure he doesn't work for that agency again. Look at the times. The dates. The boy claims never to have taken a lunch hour!

Linda But he did. Sometimes longer than an hour.

Dave Oh, so you admit that?

Dave laughs.

Linda What's funny?

Dave You are. You're unbelievable.

Linda Dave

Dave Linda. Do you have any idea how serious this is?

Linda I do. I'm just not sure what you want me to say. Obviously I didn't do this on purpose.

Dave Is it obvious?

Linda I should have thought so.

Dave It's fraud. Actually. Is what it is.

Linda I agree!

Dave And you don't think there's any reason I should be especially concerned about the fact that you've signed off on all this? You can't think of anything
    anything at all regarding you and this this Luke
    that I should know about? Because certain information has reached my ears Linda and aside from the fact that you're a married woman
    a mother
    aside from the fact that he's young enough to be your son

Linda Who is?

Dave quite aside from any of that
    I find it extremely concerning that along with the discovery that you've been having a relationship with this boy

Linda I've what?

Dave I suddenly find out he's been paid almost twice what he should have been.

Linda I haven't been having a relationship with him.

Dave Oh Linda.

Linda Who told you that?

Dave It's not important.

Linda It's also not true. I want to know who said it. Who said it?

Dave I'm asking the questions, OK? Look at that information again and tell me you're in a position to be asking the questions. You've signed off on thousands of pounds. Thousands. At a time when the company is already in trouble.

Linda Maybe I have, but if I have it was an accident. Yes maybe I'm guilty of of of being neglectful or something but not of fraud! Dave! You know me!

Dave I thought I did. Now I'm not so sure.

Linda What is this?

Dave First you make a complete fool of yourself in front of the Board. I ask you to take some time out to get your head together. You refuse. Then I find out you're carrying on with this boy like a what's the word? Cougar.

Linda I'm not / carrying on with anyone!

Dave And now this disaster with the timesheets!

Linda Dave –

Dave No you know what? I'm not even going to get angry. There's no point, is there? I can have all the feelings I want about this, it isn't going to change anything. You know the person I feel really sorry for is Neil.

Linda Neil?

Dave On the occasions I've met him I've found him to be utterly charming. And you're damn lucky I'm an honourable man

damn lucky
because if Neil saw those emails
if he found out what you've been doing
he'd be devastated. And please don't look at me like
that. You know exactly what I'm talking about.

Linda What emails?

Dave clicks something on his computer. Clears his throat.

Dave 'Hi sexy. Thanks for a good time earlier. Can't stop thinking about you naked'.

A high-pitched noise whines loudly. Linda grabs her head.

Linda I don't understand.

Dave You want me to read the rest?

Beat.

How could you be so stupid? A woman of your age.

Linda walks away from Dave. She stands facing away from him.

That's not the worst of it I'm afraid. Apparently everyone else at the company has also received a copy of these emails. In fact there's a whole thread of replies some of which are
well, put it this way the sales boys have had a field day. Someone's got hold of Photoshop. I won't trouble you with the details. I think you'd find them very upsetting. Amy certainly did. She was deeply concerned for your well-being. So she sent them on to me.

Linda does not look at him.

Linda I don't understand. That's
those were private. They were
private.

Pause.

Eventually Linda turns round.

Dave. Listen to me. I don't know how that happened or
    what it means but
    whatever that is, it has nothing
    nothing
    to do with my work
    this has nothing to do with my ability to perform /my
job this is

Dave Stop, will you? Just stop! / Stop!

Linda I can't stop, don't you understand, that's the whole
    I don't want to stop I'm not ready to stop! Please
    please don't make me stop!

Dave turns away from her.

Beat.

Dave (*quietly*) It's gone too far.

Linda What did you say? I didn't hear you.

Dave All you had to do was support my decision and be
a team player. After everything I've done for you, that's
all I asked. But you couldn't do it, could you? You've
always got to be centre stage.

Linda Please . . .

Dave If you resign now

Beat.

Linda covers her face with her hands.

if you resign now I think we can probably push all this
under the carpet. True Beauty can stand for itself and it
won't be tainted by
    well. The shadow of corruption.

Linda And if I don't?

Beat.

Dave I mean if you don't? If you don't then we'll have to investigate the fraud. The sexual scandal. I think it's a potentially devastating course of action, yes, for the company but more importantly for you. You've got your kids to think about. You wouldn't want to put them through all that, I'm sure. I know how those girls look up to you.

Beat.

You can take a bit of time to think about it, OK?

Linda How much time?

Dave Lunchtime?

Beat.

OK, for old times' sake I'll give you till the end of the day. But that's it. Either I have that resignation letter on my desk at five p.m. or
  well . . . I've made my point.

Beat.

I know I can rely on you, Linda. Given how much you care about this company and about our reputation? I know I can rely on you to do the right thing.

ELEVEN

Bridget's audition.

Bridget is wearing an old-man costume.
  Including a large beard.

Behind her, the sound of the hurricane builds.

Bridget Blow winds and crack your cheeks!
   Rage!
   Blow!
   Singe my white head! And thou, all-shaking thunder
   uh
   Thou all-shaking thunder and
   and

   Beat.

I'm so sorry. I did it wrong. Can I have another go?

TWELVE

Linda's office.

Linda returns to her office.

She stands in the middle of the room for a moment. Outside the storm rages.

Suddenly, Linda cries out.

She goes to the shelf of bottles and knocks everything off the shelf.

She destroys anything in her path, making noises of despair and confusion.

She kicks off her shoes. Rips at her tights.

She rips the jacket off her dress suit. Underneath a silk blouse, stained with sweat.

She goes to the window, opens it.

She lets the storm in.

THIRTEEN

A studenty house.
Luke and Alice stand by a window, smoking a spliff.
A large rucksack and a suitcase nearby.

Outside, the wind.

Alice Thanks for this. I really appreciate it. If I'd had to stay one more day at my mum's I might actually have gone mad. I mean
   of course I should be able to be at peace in any location it's just
   well
   this is very cool of you. Thank you. What time's your flight?

Luke I should go in a few. Finish this first.

Alice You think they'll fly in this weather?

Luke No idea.

Alice Your plane might get blown away.

Luke I doubt it.

Alice I know.

   She smiles at him.

   I'll see you out there though?

Luke Sure.

Alice And thanks for this. I really appreciate it.

Luke No worries. 'Sarah'.

   Alice laughs.

Alice I like it. I think it's anonymous. 'Hi, I'm Sarah. Pleased to meet you.'

Luke And Sarah's much better-looking than Alice.

Alice What?

Luke She doesn't wear that weird old jumpsuit.

Alice I mean. OK.

Beat.

Luke What?

Alice Nothing, it's just I don't want to be valued according to my physical appearance. I didn't think we did that. In Big Wisdom.

Luke Chill out. It was meant to be a compliment!

Alice Well I don't enjoy compliments! Please don't give me 'compliments'!

Luke Sure. Hey. Let's not have an argument OK? Remember every time an angry feeling comes up? Stop trying to chase it or change it. Let it flow on.

He does a little action with his hand, to indicate flowing on. Then coughs.

He passes the spliff back to Alice. Then:

You know what I think your biggest lessons will be?

Alice Go on.

Luke Stillness and acceptance. Those are two qualities you really need to work on. You've got to stop fighting and learn to surrender.

Alice Stillness / and acceptance.

Luke Shhhh. Hush now. Just be quiet.

FOURTEEN

Linda sits amid the devastation in her office.

Amy is standing in the doorway.

Amy Oh my God!

> *Beat.*

> *Linda looks up.*

What happened?
  Linda?
  Are you OK?

Linda I'm just

Amy What's going on?

Linda I'm having a sort-out in my office.

> *Beat.*

Amy I came to

> *Beat.*

maybe it's not a good time.

Linda Wait!
  I need to talk to you.

> *Beat.*

Dave said
  he said you were the one
  you saw those
  what d'you call 'ems. You sent them to Dave.
  Emails.

> *Beat.*

Amy They got sent round.

I felt so sorry for you. I thought Dave should know. I hope that was OK.

Linda He wants me to write a letter.

Amy OK.

Linda My resignation.

Amy No!

Linda I've got till five o'clock.

Amy What are you going to do?

Linda Shut the door. I don't want them to hear.

Amy Who?

Linda I need to tell you something. It's important.

Amy What is it?

Linda It's about Dave. Shut the door.

Amy OK.

Amy shuts the door.

What about him?

Linda Did you know this used to be his office?

Amy No?

Linda Because it's the best one. The best view. The view you like. Out on to the river. We met in that pub. Look. Down there. Did you know that? He fancied me. I wouldn't put out so he offered me a job. Typist. I'd come into this very room to hand him letters I'd typed so badly you could barely read them. But he wanted to spend time with me so he kept me on. Eventually we got talking about ideas, he hired me to do some marketing. Spent even more time with me then, didn't he? When True Beauty really took off he gave me this office. He said I deserved it. He said I was brilliant. And I believed it. But now I realise

I'll never know, will I? What I actually earned. What I deserved. What I was worth. And what I got just because Dave wanted to fuck me. I wish I could start again. You know? Find out for sure.

She goes over to the door.

He'll probably give you this office when I'm gone. But then you'll never know either. Don't you think that's sad?

Amy Excuse me?

Linda I'm just saying. That's the price you pay for being beautiful. Oh, when you're young you think it's a gift. You think you're lucky. And then one day you wake up and you realise

it was all an illusion.

Amy Um. I've got a first-class degree from Bristol University. So. I find it kind of offensive what you're implying. Actually.

Linda They tell you it's nature. But maybe it's not nature. Maybe it comes down to one single

fundamental truth

they're not really interested in us. See?

They're not interested. In our minds. In our ideas. In what we have to offer. They don't enjoy listening to us. Not really. They only pretend to listen as long as they want to fuck you. And why do they want to fuck you?

Amy I'm finding this quite upsetting.

Linda When you're young they want to fuck you so they can control you. But as soon as you start to get older

just as soon as you really begin to feel like a person

they take it all away.

Amy I'd like to leave now please. I'm not enjoying this conversation.

Linda Dave thinks I don't like you. Why?

Amy Maybe because you don't like me?

Linda But I've always liked you. I saw myself in you.

Amy I don't think so.

Linda You never liked me though. Did you? That little speech about how much you admire me? You didn't mean it.

Amy Can you open the door, please?

Linda Maybe you see yourself in me too. Maybe that's why I make you uncomfortable. Do I make you uncomfortable?

Amy Right now you do.

Linda There's so much to look forward to isn't there? At your age.

Amy Open the door, Linda.

Linda I've always been very good at looking forwards. I think it's one of the things that makes me good at marketing. I like imagining things. Of course I've always enjoyed looking back too. The trouble is
   right now
   at this exact moment
I'm having terrible difficulty doing either. I can't look back because as it turns out this whole time I thought I was helping my daughters
   I've been hurting them. And I can't look forwards because
   if I'm not here. Making the world a better place. Then who am I? I looked in the mirror last night and I suddenly saw
   I saw myself the way the world sees me. The way you see me. And I don't know what to do about that. I don't know how to change it.

Amy I'm going to start screaming.

Linda Maybe if I throw myself off the roof of the building maybe they'll listen. Do you think?

Linda laughs.

Amy Get out of the way.

Linda Maybe if I'm dead
they'll have to change the campaign back to how it was you know
out of respect?

Amy I don't know.

Linda But then again maybe they won't. Maybe they'll hate me even more. How can a mother abandon her children? they'll say. We can't understand it. We'd never do that. Not us.

Amy Linda?

Linda I spent the last twenty-five years being terrified of dying in case my children had no one to look after them and now
now all I want to do is die
but I can't because I feel too guilty. Why do I always have to think about other people? Doesn't there come a time in your life where you stop expecting your mother to do everything for you?

Amy I don't know, Linda. Let's get out of here and you can go ask your children.

Linda They don't want to talk to me.

Amy OK then we'll find someone else.

Linda I could try and keep going, couldn't I? Brazen it out!

Amy Just

Linda Or I could give up. Resign. Accept I've been defeated.

Amy Can anyone hear me?

Linda Or I could kill myself. Maybe / actually

Amy She's keeping me in here!

Linda serve some / purpose but

Amy I can't / get out!

Linda also be blamed for ruining my daughters' lives.

Amy Hello?

Linda Or . . . maybe there's another option.

Amy I don't care! OK? I don't want to listen to this any more!

Linda To take my revenge.

Amy Just stop, OK?

Linda On you. Not just for me. For my daughter.

Amy Revenge for what? I don't even know your daughter!

Linda Which would be more difficult? Killing myself or killing you? Or is it the same thing?

Amy This isn't funny!

Linda Maybe it's the only way I actually can make the world a better place.

Amy I've had enough of this. Hey! / Somebody!

Linda I think I'll choke you.

Amy Is there anyone there?

Linda I'll choke you till you're unconscious and then push you out the window.

Amy You keep the fuck away from me!
If you lay one finger on me, Linda, I swear to God –

*As Linda talks she approaches Amy. Amy tries to
move to the door but Linda grabs her by the hair,
shoves her and puts her hands around her throat.
Amy struggles but Linda is stronger. As:*

Linda I'm doing you a favour, that's what you've got to
remember, Amy. Come here. Hey –

Amy Ow!

Linda Stop that.

Amy Let go!

Amy cries out. But Linda has her in a vice-like grip.

Linda Think about it. You'll be famous. All those photos
of you on the front page of the paper. They'll print a lot
of pictures, you know, they always do when a pretty
young woman dies. And best of all – you'll never get old.

Amy Get off me!

*Linda grabs Amy round the throat. Amy gasps and
gurgles. Her legs go wild. Linda is unshakeable.*

(Linda! / Please! You're hurting me! I can't breathe!)

Linda You can die, Amy. Just like any other human
being. Because underneath your pretty skin you're blood
and muscle and bones and vital organs pumping fluid and
all that can be snuffed out in a second.

Amy (Please!)

Linda Are you worried about crow's feet now?
Are you worried about fine lines?
Are you worried about getting older?
Do you want to live to turn thirty?

Amy (Yes.)

Linda You want to live to be my age don't you?
Older even?

Amy (Yes.)

Linda You do?

Amy (Yes! Please, Linda. Please!)

Linda lets Amy go.

Linda I can't do it.

*Amy falls to the floor, gasping and coughing. Maybe
she's a bit sick or something. Linda staggers backwards.
Her breathing has gone strange.*

I can't do it. I'm so sorry. I can't do it. Not even for my
daughter's sake. You see? Not even for her. I'm sorry.

*Amy crawls away, clutching her throat. Trying to
recover.*

I'm so sorry, Alice. I let you down.

Linda walks away, over to the window.

There is a pause.

At least you can have this office now. That's nice for you
isn't it?

Beat.

And you're right. It's the most fabulous view.

Beat.

Oh look, there's a woman on the bridge putting her
umbrella up. Why do people do that? Ha. Look. It's
gone. Wind lifted it right out of her hands.

FIFTEEN

Home. Evening.

Neil and Bridget sit at the table.

Bridget That was her, wasn't it? 'Stevie'.

Neil It sounds like it.

Bridget She's like, the same age as Alice.

Neil A little bit older.

Bridget Why did she come to see Mum?

Neil I don't know. I haven't spoken to her. I have no idea.

Bridget Why didn't Mum tell me?

Neil I don't know. She probably wanted to protect you.

Bridget Protect me from what?

Neil What an idiot your old man is.

Bridget I shouted at her.

Neil Who?

Bridget Mum. Before I called you
    I was so angry. I said all this mean stuff to her because it was like. She was there, you know? No one else was there and I just needed to be angry. I said I wanted her to leave. She won't, will she?

Neil Course not.

Bridget Mum's the most amazing woman in the world. Isn't she?

Neil I think so.

Bridget She's strong and she's funny and she's brave. And she cares about us.

Neil She does.

Bridget I had this weird moment when I was sitting in the room
    waiting to go in
    I was in my costume and there was these other girls there. They'd made themselves look pretty and they were all skinny and good-looking and doing Cordelia or Ophelia and I was there with a stupid beard on and at first I felt like a twat, you know? But then I started feeling like
    like I actually was him. And they were my daughters
    and I thought about what it must be like to have a daughter
    and about how Mum is like
    how she didn't have an easy life but she's still done amazing things and I remembered all the stuff I said to her this morning and how
    there isn't a person in the whole world who I love
    who I love like I love her. I love her so much it hurts. And I started feeling what it must be like to have your own daughter turn on you like I did this morning
    to have the people you love most betray you
    for reasons you can't understand because you've only ever done your best
    and after that I couldn't really concentrate on the stupid audition because all I could think about was getting home and telling Mum I love her. More than anyone. And how special and beautiful and perfect she is.

Neil I need to tell her the same thing.

Bridget Sometimes I just forget how lucky I am to have her.

Neil We won't forget again. Shall we make a pact? Let's make a pact. We won't ever take her for granted
    ever again. Deal?

Bridget Deal.

Beat.

Neil She should be on her way home by now. Do you think?

Bridget checks the time.

Bridget Hope so.

Neil Maybe I'll give her a call. Check she's on her way.

SIXTEEN

Linda's office.

Linda is writing the last bit of a letter.

She signs it. Puts it in an envelope. Leaves it on her desk.

She applies a lick of lipstick and a generous dollop of Hi-Beautiful. She fouffs her hair and puts her shoes on. She picks up her bag.

She goes over to the window.

A beat.

She opens the window.

The storm gusts in. Takes her breath away. She staggers back a few steps.

On the table, her phone rings. It plays a little tune. Vibrates around a little.
   She looks at it.
   Decides not to answer.

The ringing stops.

She steps out on to the ledge.

Stevie plays her gig.

She sings P. J. Harvey, 'Who Will Love Me Now?'
   She does well.

The applause for Stevie's gig turns into:

A stage, in a spotlight.
   Ten years ago.

Linda is wearing a glittery dress. Different hair.
   She clutches her award.
   The applause dies down.

Linda Wow. Thank you. This is just
   incredible. Thank you. OK so. Sorry, uh
   I really wasn't expecting this. What do I want to say?
   Uh. I want to thank my colleagues at Swan who are
   the most inspirational supportive
   innovative and bloody brilliant bunch of people.
Kenina. Susan. My husband Neil who is the most
amazingly gorgeous, lovely, understanding bloke a girl
could ask for – Neil I love you. To everyone who's
bought a Swan beauty product after seeing or hearing
about this campaign. Thank you. So much. For
understanding what it's all about and what we're trying
to do.

   *She takes a deep breath. Composes herself. Goes
   serious.*

The True Beauty campaign is an idea which to many
people still seems like something too bold. Too different.

Too audacious to even contemplate. But it's a campaign we all passionately – passionately – believe in. Something we've put ourselves on the line for because at Swan we believe women have had enough of being told how they 'should' look. We believe the future lies in expanding our notions of what beauty is so that the media is more up to date with how we as human beings feel inside. Which is to say

those whom we love

we find beautiful. We believe the staggering success of this campaign should tell us, as an industry, that women are sick of the waif-like models which the last decade brought and which we continue to see in mainstream advertising. Women are ready to move forwards. We've entered a brand-new century, people. Let's act like it, shall we?

A round of applause and cheers from the audience. Linda laughs. As the applause dies down, she goes serious:

You know I can't believe what a difference ten years can make.

Beat.

I joined Swan in nineteen ninety-five as a single mother with no experience in this industry. No qualifications. And from the bottom of my heart I want to say thank you

to the man who is not only my CEO but who I am also proud to call a friend and mentor: Dave Hodges. Dave, you took a chance on me when I really didn't know anything about beauty or marketing. You admired my spirit – and – thank you for that. For seeing my potential and giving me a shot. You always listened. Always supported. I share this with you.

Beat.

And finally

I want to thank my daughters

Alice and Bridget. Bridget's still too little to understand what Mummy does. But my daughter Alice is a teenager. The media's body-image fascism is bearing down on her and her peers, with full force. Alice will be taking her GCSEs this summer. She's insanely beautiful, with a figure to die for – but Alice plans to go to university

and study medicine. She wants to be a doctor, working with children in developing countries. And I am so – so proud of her for that. Because my daughter is a young woman who refuses to be defined by her outward appearance. And ten years from now, I truly believe, the wider culture will be able to do the same. This award is a sign

a symbol if you like
that for us women
and for our daughters
things are finally
finally
getting better.

The End.